A captivating story of hope a

Margaret Feinberg, author of *Fight Back* ~~~~~

I had no intention to sit down and read this book cover to cover in one sitting, but Candice drew me into her story from the opening chapter. She writes so honestly about the painful childhood memories and wounds left by her father. I found myself in awe of her strength and resilience. *The Con Man's Daughter* is a journey of hope, redemption, and the relentless love of a God who pursues us beyond the ends of the earth. You will be captivated.

Melanie Shankle, *New York Times* bestselling
author of *Nobody's Cuter Than You*

Awesome read. Awesome story. God can always take a mess and make it his message. Candice weathered some incredible storms—this is a must-read! If Candice can make it, anyone can. Once I began to read, I couldn't put it down! Hope, help, and healing are in these pages. Take the journey with Candice!

Ken Freeman, author, evangelist, and motivational speaker

From the first 120 mph wild ride Candice Curry takes with her earthly father to the first frightened whispered prayer to her heavenly one, I felt like a passenger in the speeding sports car of her life journey. She tells a story of heartbreak and redemption with an emotional yet humorous voice that both draws the reader in and leaves her changed.

Jenny Rapson, editor, ForEveryMom.com

*The Con Man's Daughter* is a wild ride full of brokenness and pain, beauty and redemption. You will laugh and cry. You will want to hold little Candice in your arms and speak belovedness over her. You will cheer for her in her bravery and resilience and weep for her in her pain. Candice bravely shares the real truths of what it was like to grow up with a broken father and how it affected her. She doesn't try to wrap things up in a pretty bow or avoid the hard parts, but shares with authenticity how God met her in the brokenness and brought about healing and redemption. It is full of unspeakable pain, unfathomable grace, unpredictable redemption, and breathtaking beauty.

Brandi Lea, US founder and director,
Beauty for Ashes Uganda

Candice Curry has an incredible gift of sharing her story with grace, authenticity, and humbleness. I could not put this book down, and when I did, I could not stop thinking about what could possibly happen next. Her life and her story got into my head, but even more so, into my heart. There were parts of her story that broke my heart, and I found myself weeping for her loss. But God. As strong as the pain is in these chapters, redemption runs stronger. In her story she has given us a view of her own transformation—from bitterness to forgiveness. If God can help her to forgive the deepest, darkest wounds of her soul, then, surely, he can help any of us walk through forgiveness and experience what she has penned in these pages . . . freedom. Share *your* story and set others free.

Celeste Barnard, author and speaker

# THE
# CON MAN'S
# DAUGHTER

# THE
# CON MAN'S
# DAUGHTER

A Story of Lies, Desperation,
and Finding God

## CANDICE CURRY

**BakerBooks**
*a division of Baker Publishing Group*
Grand Rapids, Michigan

Published by Baker Books
a division of Baker Publishing Group
P.O. Box 6287, Grand Rapids, MI 49516-6287
www.bakerbooks.com

Printed in the United States of America

Library of Congress Cataloging-in-Publication Data is on file at the Library of Congress, Washington, DC.

ISBN 978-0-8010-1961-6

Some names and details of the people and situations described in this book have been changed or presented in composite form in order to ensure the privacy of those with whom the author has worked.

Author is represented by ChristopherFerebee.com, Attorney and Literary Agent.

17  18  19  20  21  22  23      7  6  5  4  3  2  1

To my mom—You're the behind-the-scenes hero and always have been. You've sacrificed over and over to make sure I've always had what I need and have given me as many of my wants as you could. For that I am forever grateful. Thank you for being my loudest cheerleader and my one and only Shema Shema.

To Jordan—My entire life has been filled with belly laughs and a sense of security because you're the greatest big brother a girl could ask for. To sum it all up: "Turn out the lights, I lost my necklace."

To Brandon—You're my entire world, for better or worse, in sickness and in health, till death do us part. No matter what we've walked through or what waits for us in the future, I wouldn't want to do it with anyone else. Thank you for your patience, support, and humor. You're my Kevin Arnold.

# CONTENTS

# BEFORE WE BEGIN

Redemption is the promise of a gift that follows brokenness. While not all roads to redemption are the same, we all have broken areas in our lives.

As a little girl, I would stick my hand in the back pocket of my dad's Levi jeans so I wouldn't get lost when we were out in public. He was my guide. I didn't have to look up; I knew he was there. I blindly followed his lead. Where he went I went, with a naive confidence that he would not steer me wrong. He was my dad after all; I knew nothing else but to trust him. I was always the little girl with her hand in my father's pocket.

As the years went on and I grew taller and slightly wiser, I started to lift my gaze from his feet to the road ahead and realized the path he had me on was full of lies and deceit. His path was paved with drugs and manipulation, and as a result he was laying down those same bricks for me.

My father was involved with the FBI for things I'll never know. My best guess, from information I've gathered, is that he did work for them after being caught in one of his con man games. In return for his cooperation, he was spared prosecution. I remember the FBI coming to my house when I was a little girl and being told to go to the other room while he talked to the men in suits. My childhood was filled with moments like that, strange people showing up or calling the house trying to track my dad down. Maybe that's why we lived in seventeen different houses before I finished high school.

His con man ways meant we drove stolen cars, lived in stolen houses, and shopped and dined on "borrowed" credit cards. This led to a lifestyle of constantly looking over our shoulders. Even as small children, my brother and I intuitively knew something was wrong and that something bad could happen at any time.

As you can imagine, living with secrets and drug use meant my dad was often on edge. We never knew what to expect with him and feared which version of our dad would walk through the door. It was either the funny and playful dad that let us to do whatever we wanted or the dad that was high on whatever he could get his hands on and who would torture us with his words. The sneaky lifestyle I was exposed to, as well as the mental and emotional abuse I endured at the hands of my father, left deep scars I've dealt with for most of my life.

As children we look to our parents to measure our value and find our worth. When that source is missing or broken or painful, we often search desperately to find meaning through other earthly things. We dive into unhealthy relationships in an effort to make us feel complete and, unfortunately, often end up self-destructing, which only causes more pain and brokenness.

I spent most of my life begging for approval from my father. I cried out to him instead of crying out to the One who could heal me. I stamped a label on myself very early on, a label I felt my father handed to me. I was worthless and had no real value. No one could possibly love me for who I truly was, and there could be no redeeming value in me. I built a wall. It took me years to stack each brick, one on top of the other, until they reached high enough to protect me from anyone finding out what was deep inside of me. I took on my father's sins as my own and carried them with me everywhere I went.

But, like all of us, I had a choice to make. I could hang on to everything I had been through, let it pull me down and become my identity, or I could be set free from it and find a way to forgive.

Forgiveness is a hard choice to make; it takes a strength we do not have on our own. I make a daily choice not only to forgive the sins against me but also to forgive myself for where I've been and what I've done. God didn't create me to be a victim, beat down and broken. He made me to be his hands and feet and to share with others how healing it is to forgive and hand yourself over to his will for your life.

God can work through any circumstance and heal what's been shattered. He shines through all of our broken pieces.

This is my story.

# ONE

# The Devil Inside

I could hear my name being called, but I was stuck somewhere between a dream and reality. As it got louder I could feel myself trying to wake up and escape the nightmare, not realizing my reality wouldn't be much different. I turned over to face where the noise was coming from and barely cracked one eye open, just enough to read my alarm clock. It was 1:37 a.m. I heard my name again. This had to be part of my nightmare. My alarm was set to go off in five hours, and I was desperate for a full night of sleep.

"Candice, get up."

I finally snapped to and sat up in bed to discover my dad sitting next to me, covered in sweat, telling me we had to leave.

At thirteen, I had learned not to question him or his motives, and I knew well enough to just go along with whatever it was he was up to. But now? Really? It was almost two in the morning! This wasn't right and I knew it. Whatever it was we were going to do or wherever it was we were headed, it wasn't going to lead to anything good.

I mumbled something under my breath and put two feet on the floor. Dizziness rushed to my head from getting up so quickly, and I complained to my dad, who was rushing about frantically looking for absolutely nothing. I knew he didn't hear a word I said. Since I already had on an oversized T-shirt, I grabbed a pair of sweatpants and tennis shoes. There was no need to pack a bag. This trip wouldn't be long; I could tell by the look in his eyes and the fact that all he had in his possession was a set of car keys and a pack of cigarettes. I wanted to take one of the cigarettes out, light it for him, and tell him to sit down and relax. As a matter of fact, I wanted to take one of those cigarettes out, light it for myself, and tell my dad I wasn't going anywhere. I pictured myself with a red ember glowing from one side of my mouth with a look in my eye that said I didn't have time for this. On more than one occasion I had snuck one of those cigarettes, and my friends and I smoked it as if we were the coolest kids on the block. It usually ended with us either throwing up or left with a pounding headache. But we looked cool. He probably knew each time we did it, but he didn't care. Confronting me about it would require him to discipline me, and he wasn't able to do that. His parenting was crippled by his quest to be cool.

I'm not sure I ever viewed him as an authority figure in my life. He was my dad, of course, but he was a far cry from a father. Most of the time, it felt like I was caring for him instead of the other way around. He married my mom when they were both teenagers and had my brother shortly after. I came along two years after that. We were never the Cleavers. My mom went to college and nursing school when we were young and then had the pressure of being the breadwinner for the family. She had to work long, hard hours because my dad had never held a job a day in his life, and had no intention of getting one. In order to support our family, my mom often worked the overnight shift because it paid better. Unfortunately, this left my brother and me in the care of my dad, who quite honestly needed a babysitter himself. He lived in his own world, which often left my brother and me with the option to either play along or get left behind. On this night in particular, I decided to play along.

Parked in our driveway was a vintage convertible Alfa Romeo Spider—the most beautiful two-seater sports car I had ever seen. The outside was snuggled in a coat of deep red paint and the interior was a cloud of tan leather. There wasn't a single flaw on the car, not a scratch or dent anywhere to be seen, and it made me think it had just left the production line. I felt sorry for the owner who was no doubt looking for it, but I was also excited to get to ride in it. My dad had a way of borrowing things and never returning them. That's how he had acquired the fancy sports car that was about to take me on an adventure. Little did I know this adventure would be the start of my quest to rid the sense of worthlessness that slowly grew inside of my soul.

We peeled out of the driveway as if it were necessary, as if we were already being followed. I'm sure in my dad's twisted head there was someone on our tail. I still had no idea where we were headed, and if I thought for one second that God knew who I was I would have said a prayer. But I was certain that God didn't know girls like me. He knew only the good girls, the ones that showed up in his church on Sundays and made all the right choices throughout the rest of the week. He didn't know the girl whose own dad didn't value her.

I strained to hear God's voice in my ear but only heard Satan whisper how much he loved me.

By the time we reached the highway my dad was having a full-blown panic attack. The sweat that seeped from his pores was making his clothes wet, and he smelled like something I couldn't identify. I learned later in life that the smell was a combination of cocaine and cologne. It was a ritual for him to douse himself in Canoe cologne before he left the house. He might as well have showered in it because he was literally wet with it by the time he was done spraying. The stench made me gag. He lowered the top of the convertible to help with the intense heat he was giving off in the small space of the car, and the fresh air woke me up and made both of us fully alert. As soon as we got on the highway and headed north, I knew exactly where we were going. What I didn't know was why it was so urgent to leave at 2:00 a.m. I wasn't alarmed by all the craziness going on in the middle of the night; this sort of thing had become normal and frequent. I learned to go with it and enjoy the excitement of being out in the dark of night, wondering if we were going to get caught doing something we weren't supposed to.

The howling of the wind started to drown out my dad's rambling, and my eyes focused on the road that was so close to me I could almost reach out and touch it. I wanted to run my fingers alongside as we sped down the highway, the way I did when we were in our boat and I could feel the water next to us. The thought of being in the boat with sunshine on my face made me smile, but I knew this would not be a trip where we lowered the boat into the water. I tried to mentally remove myself from the speeding car and place myself in the fresh water. It was impossible. We were going so fast that the broken white stripes on the highway blurred to form one solid line, and the trees bravely lining the highway became a smear of green that prevented me from seeing beyond the confines of the road. In that moment I had zero fear of the speed we had managed to reach. I wasn't worried about suddenly going into a tailspin or losing control. All control had already been lost, and I surrendered to the fact that whatever happened from here on out was not in my hands. Unfortunately, my trust had to be placed in the adult who was in the driver's seat, the one who was supposed to protect me at all costs.

As we reached a speed of 120 miles per hour, a police officer passed us going in the opposite direction. We must have been like a mosquito that buzzes by your face and that you can't seem to track afterward. My dad's body tensed up. I felt a sense of relief. There was no way that officer wasn't going to make a U-turn and flip his lights on. My body was contorted in the passenger seat so that I could turn around and watch for his lights behind us. The extremely small interior of the car made it hard to turn around. There was no seat-belt law, and my dad was too cool for us to be wearing them. We were full speed ahead and, without a single glance in his rearview mirror, my dad's foot pressed harder on the accelerator. He let me know that if I saw lights behind us we were without a doubt headed to jail.

We?

We were headed to jail?

Had I somehow gone from an innocent passenger to an accomplice? I was anything but a naive child, and I assumed there was something in the car that would send him straight to jail. What I didn't realize was that the one thing in the car that wasn't supposed to be there was me. I was supposed to be home in bed, getting enough sleep to make it through school the next day, not driving to the lake in the middle of the night.

My dad had one cassette tape in the car and we listened to it endlessly. Once we reached the end of side A, he would flip it over and start side B. Blaring from the speakers was INXS, my dad's favorite band. "The Devil Inside" was track three on the *Kick* album, and as I sang along to the music I wondered if Michael Hutchence was talking about me or my dad.

The lights of a police car never followed us and it disappointed me. I asked my dad where I would go if they put him in jail. Would I have to go to the women's jail without him and would they put me in a cell? I was serious. I had no idea what happened to the child when someone got arrested. Would they consider me a child? Would I get handcuffed? My questions almost irritated him, and he gave me short answers that didn't ease the pain that was growing in the pit of my stomach. I imagined arriving at the jail, not knowing where they had taken my dad, and the officer telling me I had one phone call. I debated about my imaginary phone call and decided that I wouldn't call my mom. I wouldn't want her to know we had snuck out. I never wanted to get my dad in trouble and I never wanted to upset my mom, so I omitted the truth to her on more than one occasion. Maybe subconsciously it was to protect her more than it was to protect my dad. In the end, I decided I would pass on the one phone call and just sit in the lobby and wait until my dad was free again. I also secretly wished we would get pulled over so that some sort of alarm would go off to the fact that a child was out in the middle of the night. I wanted an officer to pull me aside and ask what I was doing out when I should be sound asleep in the comfort and safety of my home.

But the knight in shining armor in a police uniform who I envisioned pulling us over never showed. My dad kept his foot heavy on the gas pedal, and I hummed quietly to track 4, "Need You Tonight."

It seemed like hours had passed, but when I glanced at the clock it shined brightly and said that it was only 3:15. I knew that meant we were getting close to the lake house. As a little girl I would often ride to the same lake with my friend and her family. We played a game every single time we took the trip. When we were almost to the house and drove over the very last hill, a sliver of the lake would peek out between the trees and let us know that we were soon in for a fun-filled weekend on the water. The person who screamed "I see the lake" first was the winner. There wasn't a prize except for bragging rights, but we would all tense up and sit on the edge of our seats anyway, trying to see over the dashboard farther than anyone else in the car.

As my dad and I flew over that last hill I wanted to turn toward him and yell, "I see the lake first!" but I figured it was a terrible idea and would have sent my dad over the edge even further than he already was. I chose to whisper it under my breath and call myself the winner.

After flying over the highway at top speed and not caring about a single other car on the road, my dad slowed down to a snail's crawl when we reached the quaint neighborhood of the lake house. Porch lights only lit the front of the occasionally occupied lake houses. As we silently crept around curves and crawled up and down the small hills, I noticed my dad had turned off the headlights of the car. It felt like we had entered a game of cloak and daggers but had no opponent. My dad loved the idea of being hunted by the authorities and eluding them in the dead of night. It was a game he played in his head all the time. Years of drug abuse and mental illness messed with his mind and to him, he was truly living out this weird fantasy. I desperately wanted to hit the power button on his game and call it quits, but he was stuck in the on position, and there was nothing I could do but allow myself to be one of the players in the game.

We finally reached our destination and pulled into the garage of the three-story lake house that my dad had somehow gained entrance to for several months.

He was good like that. He came home with cars and diamonds in exchange for work he did on the side. We had the keys to lake houses, ranch houses, and more because of some deal he had made. Growing up I never thought anything of it; I truly believed my dad had worked for these things and that we had a right to them. By the time I was seventeen years old, we had lived in as many different houses. I assumed it was normal and that people who lived in the same house all of their lives were missing out on something.

He turned the car off and we removed ourselves from the pillow-like seats. I followed my dad inside the house like a good soldier and then watched him roam aimlessly around as if he was checking on things that needed checking on. He flipped a light switch on and off a few times, opened doors to the patio and then shut them, went upstairs, came back down, went downstairs, then came back up, and finally made his way to the master bedroom. He crawled into bed without removing a single item of clothing and passed out.

Each weekend that we had come before, I stayed on the third floor with my friends. It was a loft with multiple beds, decorated in beach and boat decor. I loved it up there, but this night was different. It was dark and big. The silence was frightening. I chose to kick off my shoes and crawl into bed next to my dad under the delusion that he could protect me if something happened. The rest of the night (and morning) was completely uneventful except for my dad snoring so loud that it kept me from getting any sleep.

At 7:00 a.m. my dad shot out of bed as if someone had hit the eject button underneath him. There was a shocked yet glazed look in his eyes that I was all too familiar with, and I knew that he was not the same dad that drove me here the night before.

"What are you doing here?"

"You drove us here last night!"

"Who?"

"You."

"Why?"

"I don't know, Dad."

"Get in the car. Your mother is going to kill me."

My friends were miles away, eating breakfast with their families. Their lunches were packed, homework finished, and backpacks checked. Their parents were driving them to school, making sure they arrived safely and headed into school to start their day as seventh graders.

I was waking up next to my dad who had no recollection whatsoever of the night before. It was a complete blackout for him. Fueled by drugs and alcohol, he had driven me miles away from the safety of my home and didn't remember a minute of it. He had reached speeds of 120 miles an hour the night before, yet he had no memory of even driving.

For the first time in my life I realized I wasn't like other kids my age. It was the first time I knew that my dad, although tons of fun, was an extremely irresponsible adult and had complete disregard for me not only as his daughter but also as a human being in general. Nothing was the same for me after that day. I never again viewed my dad as a protector, and I never again felt special in his eyes. He threw away my worth that day, and it has taken more than half my life and what has felt like an eternity of excruciating pain to get it back.

My dad's actions that night hardened a small corner of my heart that, over time, would spread across the rest of my heart like the plague. The pain created a hole in me that I would spend the next twenty years filling with things that would hurt me in ways that only stole more of my worth. I didn't know that God knew my name. I didn't think he could possibly love a girl like me, and he definitely couldn't treasure me as his child.

It took what felt like a lifetime to understand that God's hand was in all the moments of my life and that he would use everything to redeem my story and bless me with things I didn't think were possible. God would take that night I spent with my dad, hours away from home in a stolen house, and turn it into something precious.

Sadly, that night didn't stop me from craving my dad's attention, approval, and affection. I spent years searching for self-worth through him, ultimately finding freedom in the only Father capable of giving it.

# TWO

# Daddy's Little Girl

As a little girl I thought my dad was some sort of financial wizard. I watched as people sought him out to help with legal and money woes and believed he was a legal genius. In one of my third-grade classrooms, each student had to stand up and say what our dad did for a living. This was my shining moment to brag about him. I wondered if the teacher had created the assignment just to see how it was that my family had a garage of rotating, obscenely expensive cars or how we managed to live in a new home every year.

I sat patiently as each child stood up and told about their dad's job, eager to tell them all about how special my dad was. I listened with a grin as each one proudly announced that their dad was a lawyer, a doctor, a manager at our local grocery store, or a school bus driver. I saw how excited each classmate was and how proud they were of their dad. I was ready to brag about mine. When it was my turn, I straightened out the crease in my shirt, cleared my throat to make sure everyone in the room could hear me, stood up, and proudly announced that my dad was a bookie. My teacher smiled at me with a slightly furrowed brow while I stood tall with my chin held high. This was my shining moment. This was the moment that I got to brag about my dad to the whole class and they had to listen. I was the only kid in the room whose dad was a bookie, and it made me happy that he was unique. I found myself filled with complete pride.

I had no idea what I had just said, and thankfully, none of the kids did either. I thought a bookie was someone who kept financial records for lawyers and judges. I don't know why that word stuck in my head as my dad's profession. I'm sure there had been talk of bookies needing to collect from him or something on that level, but I thought it was all on the up-and-up. Lunch in the teacher's lounge that day must have been full of giggles and concerns. My mom got a phone call from my teacher after school. I can only imagine her shock as she listened to how her daughter proudly boasted to her class that her dad was basically taking illegal bets.

## Badge of Honor

When I was nine years old my dad bought me a new T-shirt. It was blue and read *Daddy's Little Girl* in bright white letters. If my parents would have let me, I would have worn it every day for the rest of my life. It was my favorite shirt. Made of 100 percent cotton, it was the softest and most comfortable piece of clothing I had ever worn. But that's not why I loved it so much. I idolized my dad. He was handsome, smart, and the funniest person I knew. At nine years old, I thought he could do no wrong, and in my eyes he was the best dad a girl could ask for. I wanted everyone to know that I was his little girl, and somehow that shirt had become a badge of honor. I assumed all the other girls in my class were jealous that their dad hadn't gifted them with a shirt like mine. I wondered if they secretly wished my dad was theirs. I thought he was a giant, the strongest man alive. And not only was he strong, he was also a kind of smart that reached far beyond my understanding. I knew he hadn't attended college, but I also knew he had a way about him. Everyone knew he was smart; only a few knew how he used his knowledge.

Growing up I knew other dads weren't like mine. I knew he was different. If there was a prize for funniest dad, he would have been the recipient. He could make us belly laugh on a daily basis, and all my friends wanted to be around him because of the smiles he brought to their faces. He was *that* dad. He had a magnetic personality that drew everyone in. He was the dad that would honk and yell at us out the window as he pulled up to school to pick us up. When we would get to the door and reach for the handle, he would inch the car forward and we would ultimately end up chasing the car down the pick-up line. Even though my brother and I tired of it quickly, our friends loved every second of it, and that fueled Dad to keep it up. He was quick-witted and had a comeback or a joke that could be inserted into any and every conversation. You couldn't help but like him and want to be around him. There was something about him that was undeniably irresistible.

If my dad was the funny bone, my mom was the backbone. She worked her fingers to the bone to support us. After staying home with my brother and me until we enrolled in elementary school, she enrolled herself in college. She put us on the bus each morning and then would go to school and submerge herself in studies until it was time to come home, cook dinner, and tuck us into bed. She was the behind-the-scenes hero, and we never realized it. We thought our dad was the champion. The dean's list boasted my mom's name when she graduated from nursing school. She took a job working nights in order to bring home more money. She was, after all, the only working parent and the sole breadwinner for our family. She quietly did whatever she had to do to make sure we were taken care of and always let us think our dad was the hero.

Whatever it was that my dad really did to bring in some form of income or provide things, he was good at it. We randomly had big-ticket items that I knew the average home couldn't afford. There was a new car in the driveway every few months or so, and more than once the emblem on the car was one that only the very rich could acquire. The day he rolled up to my school in a Rolls Royce I thought nothing of it, until the teachers questioned me about it the next day. They were curious as to what my dad did for a living and when we got that fancy new car. I wasn't allowed to use the word *bookie* anymore, so I told everyone he was a lawyer. To me it was just a car, and even though we had a rotating inventory of cars, this one was no different from all the others. I vaguely recall my mom's nervous demeanor with each new car, but I didn't understand credit and finances and thought she was tired of constantly having to get used to a different car. My brother and I wouldn't take full advantage of his car-acquiring skills until we got older and were the ones behind the wheel. We took advantage of it but also learned some hard lessons at the same time.

We moved often and randomly had the most amazing vacation homes. One season of life was spent on a thousand-acre ranch stocked with exotic game for us to hunt at will. We had the choice to either stay at the guest house, which was fancier than most homes I had ever lived in, or at the main house. The main house was like something out of a magazine, and each time someone joined us as a guest they would ooh and ahh over all its amazing features. My favorite part of the main house was the maid's quarters. Since no one else wanted to stay there, my girlfriends and I always made it our own little house for the weekend. It was like a secret hideaway that was conveniently attached to the kitchen and close to my parents' room—but just far enough away to keep our secrets. Behind the big fence was a huge area filled with untamed horses, each a different color. I dreamed of living like them, free to run in the sun all day long. They were so majestic and strong. No one maintained them, yet their coats glistened as the sun kissed down on them. Their beauty burned a hole in me. I wanted them to be mine. I wanted them to want me. I pictured myself walking up to the strong wooden fence and having each of them run up to me in excitement. It was as if my childhood fantasy of owning a horse ranch was within my grasp.

31

On one of our adventures, my cousin and I rode saddled horses and, acting like ranchers, gathered the wild horses and cornered them in a small area of the huge corral. It felt amazing to have control over these wild animals, as if they were ours and their obedience was a learned behavior. In reality, they were terrified of us. After we cornered them with no escape, they broke the fence and ran freely into the wooded acres where my brother and dad were hunting. We knew that there was no chance of getting them back on our own, so we raced our horses back to the barn, unsaddled them, and put them in their stalls. With heavy breathing and pounding hearts, we made our way to the maid's quarters and vowed to keep the entire event to ourselves. Though we heard my dad outside the house cursing up a storm, there was no way we were going to confess what we had done. The entire event was chalked up to a faulty fence, and as many horses as possible were recovered from the hunting acres and put back in the corral. We learned a hard lesson about trying to tame a wild animal. You can't force something or someone to be what they aren't and never will be.

## From the Outside Looking In

Growing up it looked and felt like we were a typical family. From the outside looking in, it seemed like we had it all. Even from the inside it looked pretty good. We had times of extreme extravagance that as kids we delighted in.

Summers were spent at the lake. Our vacation home for that season was a three-story lake house with all the bells and whistles. In the boat slot hung a vessel that only a few other people on the lake could afford. The deck of the boat was huge and could hold lots of people, but underneath the deck was the real gem. Once you got past the door that required you to duck your head and squat down, there was a bed and toilet. No one on the lake needed a toilet on their boat. There was a marina within miles no matter where you were, and your home was never that far away. The toilet on the boat was for status. The bed was also completely unnecessary, but that didn't stop my friends and me from hiding under there and creating our own little world. It was a secret clubhouse, and we didn't feel like we were missing out on anything. In addition to the overpriced boat, there were a few jet skis. It didn't matter how old you were, you got to drive them as far as you wanted and for as long as you wanted. We had zero boundaries on the lake. We spent so many hours on the water that several layers of our skin were burned to the point of deep pain.

The lake was my favorite place to be. My cousin was only four houses down from us, and we would travel back and forth between the two all summer long. I grew up at her lake house and knew every nook and cranny of it. Both houses and the yards in between gave us the right to just be kids, yet we wandered with a freedom we shouldn't have yet been granted.

## Becoming Tiny Adults Too Soon

I spent many weekends at my best friend's house and watched her dad closely. He was quiet and calm. His kids called him

sir and he garnered respect without demanding it. He went
to work before the sun came up and was home in time for
dinner. One weekend a month he would leave town to work
as a reserve for the Coast Guard. I always thought that was
a secret mission he wasn't allowed to talk about. He was a
decorated and respected man who had retired from the FBI
and continued to put in hours at the family's cab company.
Every time I walked through the door he would give me a
kind smile and greet me with "Well hello, Miss Snell," and
that was the extent of most of our conversations. The home
he generously provided for his family was my safe place. I
spent as much time in my best friend's home as I could and
made countless comforting memories inside its safety.

My best friend's dad wasn't loud like my dad, and he wasn't
constantly in our business the way my dad was. I knew he was
what a normal dad looked like. He showed me that normal
dads had a routine and consistency in order to provide for
their families. My dad was all about having fun and making
us laugh, but I secretly wanted a dad like my best friend's. I
wanted to call my dad sir and watch him leave each morning
for work and come home every night for dinner. While most
of my friends wanted a fun dad like mine, I was hiding my
jealousy over what they had. I wasn't even old enough to date
yet, but I promised myself that I would marry a man like the
one at my friend's house and not like the one at mine.

As my mom headed off to work each night, she reluctantly
left my brother and me in the care of our dad. We thought
we had scored big time, because he never enforced a bedtime and we were free to roam about doing pretty much

whatever our hearts desired. It was easier for him to parent this way—and be the cool parent—than it was for him to set any standards for us or enforce any rules. He was the guy who would randomly pull us out of school for a "family emergency" and then head to the lake. While the other kids were stuck behind a desk, we were headed toward the water. It was easier for my dad to let us skip school than it was for him to get up and take us and then make sure he was there to pick us up. At least once a month he wouldn't be able to get his head off of his pillow in the morning, so he would declare it a "Snell Holiday." Having our last name attached to the word *holiday* instantly meant that we were free to stay home with no consequences.

He was either extremely active and bouncing off the walls or could barely get off of the couch. He had been diagnosed with bipolar disorder and was a diagnosed sociopath. I don't remember him ever taking medication for either. On the days he didn't move, he handed us twenty dollars and a note for the cashier and sent us on our way to buy him cigarettes. We were allowed to keep the change, which took the embarrassment out of buying smokes for our dad.

Most nights, while my mom was at work and other kids were being tucked into bed, my dad let us stay up late watching scary movies. Or he sat with us in the kitchen talking about life. This is how I found out what being gay meant and what drugs were. I was in second grade, and back then those weren't things parents openly talked about with their kids. They were taboo subjects, and I knew that the other kids in my class weren't getting these kinds of lessons at home.

35

On one of those nights when my mom was burning the midnight oil at the hospital, my dad was wide awake and had no bedtime in sight. My dad, my brother, and I sat around the kitchen table talking about anything and everything we wanted. In the middle of the conversation my dad got up and went to the tall wooden cabinet that stood next to our over-sized console TV. He reached inside the highest cabinet, the one that would require me to pull a chair up next to it to reach it. After moving a few things around he pulled out a brown lunch sack and set it on our dining room table. The table was long, almost reaching from wall to wall, and was surrounded by eight chairs. We only ate at it on holidays or when we had company; it was reserved for special occasions. With bright eyes, my brother and I sat down and waited for him to pull out whatever treasure the sack held. We watched as he laid out bags of pills, powders, and what I thought was dried grass. Item by item he explained to us what each drug was. He detailed each illegal drug to his second and fourth grader, and then he told us that if we ever wanted to try drugs we needed to come to him first and not take drugs from anyone else.

That was our first "Say No to Drugs" lesson. In second grade, I could identify cocaine, marijuana, and a variety of pills. I don't think either my brother or I thought anything of it. My dad said a friend left the drugs at our house and that he had insisted his friend come and get them, but he had not shown up. We had no reason to believe otherwise and, to us, our dad was honest and safe. His favorite phrase was, "Don't tell your mother," and because we both respected and feared him, we never said a word, not to her or anyone else. Before we even reached middle school he had groomed us to be master secret keepers.

Most of my elementary years were spent with wool pulled over my eyes. I knew we weren't exactly a normal family, but it was normal to us. My mom explained to me that my dad was not a bookie but that he did financial work for people. My dad explained that he was a bankruptcy consultant, and when his clients couldn't pay him they would give him things like cars and lake houses. I didn't know what bankruptcy was or how my dad had acquired the knowledge to help people through it. He had barely made it out of high school and never spent a day in college. Yet he managed to help people through sticky legal situations and convince them to pay him with things. My mom continued to work as many hours as she could to make sure our family had a steady, legal income. She did the job of both parents, working full-time and making sure homework was done and projects completed. Her smiling face cheered us on at every event, and she scrambled daily to make sure all the bills were paid. Somehow, my dad continued to get all the glory.

My brother and I were both far too wise beyond our years. I attribute it to the nights we spent navigating our dad's insane parenting lessons. Long before we became teenagers, we knew the ins and outs of the world in ways children shouldn't. Because of our dad, we had seen more than most adults before we were even enrolled in high school. There was an angel and a devil perched on either of my shoulders, and far too many times the screech of the devil pounded in my ears, making it impossible to hear the sweet whispers of my angel.

I don't remember ever attending church; it simply wasn't a part of our childhood. I know at some point we joined the church in our neighborhood but not because I remember going. I have the picture our family took the day we became members. Four well-dressed and smiling people look back at me in that picture, and I can only imagine what it took for my mom to force us into taking it. I'm wearing a dress, which literally took an act of God. The picture has several tack holes in it from being moved around on the church bulletin board, but I can't recall taking the picture or ever being in the church. I wasn't taught Bible verses or made to sit through a service. We didn't meet up with other church families for potluck Sunday or have Bible studies in our home.

My mom believed in God—I know that for a fact—but church and religion just weren't part of our daily lives. She didn't display crosses in our home, and we rarely if ever prayed before we ate or went to sleep. The extent of our dinner prayer was my dad loudly stating, "Over the teeth, past the gums, watch out tummy, here it comes!" Maybe I believed in God, but I didn't believe he knew me. Or maybe I just thought he was a God for everyone else, the good people, the people with lives wrapped up in a pretty bow. I don't know how I sorted it all out when I was a little girl, but as I got older I just figured if there was a God, he hated me.

Eventually, I grew out of that blue and white *Daddy's Little Girl* T-shirt and had the wool removed from my eyes.

# THREE

# Turkey Pop-Tart Sandwiches

Our tight family of four began to fall apart piece by piece, and my dad's actions grew even wilder and more out of control. After the night he had driven me to the lake in a drug-fueled adventure, he never again treated me like a child and I never again saw myself as one. The relationship of father and daughter had rusted and couldn't go back to what it was before the weather took its toll. As much as my mom tried to keep everything together, it all began to crumble.

My brother and I stared at our dad across the booth at Arby's. Just the thought of dipping a curly fry in a pile of Arby's sauce made my mouth water, and I glanced again at the counter to see if our order was ready. As I tapped my feet I could hear my flip-flops stick to the floor, and I slowed my feet down so that I could make the sound stretch a little longer. The air was filled with a scent that combined old grease and cheap bathroom cleaner, and I found it oddly comforting. The five-minute fast-food wait was killing me, and I wasn't sure if it was my hunger or my brother's weird demeanor, but I knew something was slightly off. A feeling came over me that this wasn't just an outing with our dad and that a bomb was about to be dropped in our laps.

Dad finally launched the grenade while I had a mouth full of food, which I know was strategically timed. The less I could talk the better for him. In his smoothest voice, he let us know that he would be moving out and getting a home of his own. The smile never left his face as he detailed the dismantling of our little family, and the news didn't have a devastating effect on me or my brother. My brother didn't even flinch. He didn't care about the news; I could read him like a book. Honestly, by this point I didn't care either. When our parents were apart there was less fighting and mom was less stressed. This was actually a good thing for us.

A few years before, they had actually gone through with a divorce, only to remarry shortly afterward. They had set us down on our powder-pink couch to break the news. A tear immediately fell to my cheek, and I glanced over to my brother, who sat stone-cold. His eyes were completely dry. It was on that day that I started channeling his emotions and not letting anyone see my hurt. I wanted to sit stone-faced the way he was. I wanted to pretend like it didn't affect me. He pulled it off so well, and I craved to be a fraction of what he was. I remembered how just days before he had whispered to me, "Why do you cry when dad yells at us? Just laugh. He's a joke." I wanted to truly embrace not being cut to the core when my dad yelled at us because letting it eat me up inside was getting me nowhere. It would ultimately take many years for me to perfect not letting his words soak into my soul, but before that would happen, it would nearly eat me alive.

As we digested our roast beef sandwiches covered in Arby's sauce, we also digested Dad's news. Somehow he was moving into an affluent neighborhood not far from our current home. He began to verbally paint a picture for us of his new house. It boasted six bedrooms and four bathrooms. In the back-yard, just before the grass turned into woods, a black-bottom pool sparkled like a fresh-cut gem. It had all the promise of a sun-filled, water-wrinkled summer with our friends, and that's exactly how it was presented to us. Just as we had the picture of this perfect home in our heads, Dad let us know that our mom would be moving into a one-bedroom, one-bath apartment behind our neighborhood fast-food BBQ joint. For a fifteen-year-old boy and a thirteen-year-old girl, the choice seemed pretty clear. By the time we stepped foot into the parking lot, we had decided to move in with our dad. Something deep in my gut started to turn, and the thought of facing my mom was almost too much for me to think about. I knew how hard she worked for us. I knew that apartment was all she could afford. I knew she would sacrifice every-thing she had to attempt to give us everything we wanted. I knew we were about to shatter her heart.

Within days we were unpacking our suitcases in our new bedrooms. The suitcases full of clothes were all we had, and we soon realized it was about all the entire house had. My room had a twin bed and a record player and my brother's room had nothing. Absolutely nothing. As I climbed the spi-ral staircase up to his room, I couldn't decide if I was jealous or sad. He had two rooms up there and one was like a secret cave. I immediately wanted my friends to come over and have a slumber party in that room. It was a room that begged to have secrets whispered in the dark. But the bareness of it broke my heart. We had both made a poorly thought-out choice in coming to live with our dad. I wondered if my mom was wiping away tears in her little apartment. I felt selfish.

Summer kicked in days after moving in, and all of a sudden our house was filled with our friends. As the light hit my eyes one morning through the tiny rectangle window in my room, my thoughts went to the pool. I could smell bacon and eggs cooking, and that was a sure sign that dad had been up all night doing whatever it was he did on his binges. Since he was still up on his high, he was cooking breakfast tacos for me, my brother, and anyone else who had crashed at our house that night. It was the only time that he ever felt like a real dad. He was actually preparing a meal for us and, as silly as it seems, it meant that he was parenting us. The small glimpses we got of him being a parent were few and far between. Making tacos on a Saturday morning made him seem genuine and made us feel like we had a dad just like the ones we saw at our friends' houses. We shoveled the tacos in and were submerged in the pool before we had time to digest a single bite.

After one particular weekend, our house finally sat empty of company. My brother and I went to bed in his room and we assumed our dad had passed out in his. Early the next morning, I shuffled down the carpeted spiral staircase and felt the coolness of the tile as I left the bottom stair. It shocked the bottom of my feet, making me wake up a little more than I was. The kitchen was eerily quiet and oddly bare for how large it was. It was the biggest kitchen we had ever had in any of our homes, and it begged to host huge dinner parties. The cabinets seemed to reach far beyond the ceiling and could easily hold enough dinner plates and glassware for the entire neighborhood. However, behind most of them was a blank space void of anything to put food on. The refrigerator reminded me of something you would find in the kitchen of a restaurant. It was a huge stainless steel monster that was working overtime to keep only a handful of items cold.

I made my way across the living room and headed to my dad's bathroom, since it was the only one in the house that was stocked with shampoo and towels. In the living room, the sparkle of the pool outside caught my eye, and I couldn't wait for my brother and dad to wake up so we could jump in. The huge room that was designed to surround a large family with lots of seating and tables held only a single couch and nothing more. When I was a little girl the couch was covered in a soft pink material, and I thought it was made for a queen. It was the same couch that I had sat on a few years earlier and listened to my parents tell us about their divorce. At some point my mom had it recovered in a soft powder-blue fabric, and it lost its allure to me. But it was still my favorite piece of furniture. It always made it through our moves and was a comfort piece in all of our homes.

By the time I reached my dad's room I was fully awake and ready for the day. With as much grace as I could muster, I slowly turned his bedroom door handle so as to not wake him. As I tiptoed to his bathroom I glanced over at his bed and, to my shock, it was empty. A pile of wadded up blankets was carelessly thrown in the middle of the bed, and no effort had been made to clean up the room. My dad never just woke up and left without telling us, and since he never had a job to go to he was usually home when we were. But there was his bed, completely empty.

Skipping the shower altogether I ran back to my brother's room to let him know that Dad wasn't there. I was panicked. Something deep inside of me was alarming the rest of my body that everything was terribly off. We had been left alone countless times while he was out for the evening, but I knew this was different. My brother slowly emerged from under the covers, hair standing straight up, eyes slit open just enough to navigate his way around. Together we made our way back to Dad's room, since it was the only room with a phone, and tried to page him on his pager. We had been given an emergency code to use when there was trouble. My brother punched in his code, 15 911, and then hung up. Just to drive the point home, I picked up the phone and entered my code, 13 911.

And then we waited.

The phone never rang, and we spent most of the day in our dad's bed watching TV, waiting. Every few minutes throughout the day we would page him. Every page ended with 911, a signal to let him know it was an emergency.

By the time the sun tucked itself away that evening, we both knew we would be spending the night alone, without our dad. I could feel terror in my entire body. I wanted to snuggle up close to my brother, but he was a fifteen-year-old boy and they don't tend to want to cuddle with their little sisters. Our house was big with lots of windows and the thought of leaving my dad's room, for any reason, made my bones shiver. The only thing that gave us a sense of security was our one-hundred-fifty-pound Great Dane curled up at the foot of the bed. He was sweet and goofy, but the mere size of him offered us some peace of mind. My brother always played it cool, and he seemed unfazed by the fact that the day had ended and we hadn't heard a word from our dad. I tried to act like it was okay. I didn't ask him if he was scared because I didn't want him to worry about me being scared. We both stayed in the king-size bed until the scheduled TV programming ended, and we finally fell asleep.

When we woke up the next morning, the day didn't look any different from the previous one. It was quiet. There still wasn't a parent in our home, and we both knew in our guts that there might not be one for a while. My brother got up like nothing was wrong. The sun was shining and it made the house less scary. We were able to move around and not confine ourselves to our dad's room.

There had never been a day in my life that my brother showed weakness or fear in front of me. He's always been my rock. I have always known if I was with him, then I was safe. I seriously thought he was eight feet tall and the strongest person I knew. In my eyes, he was invincible.

Months before we moved into the big, empty house, my dad showed up to our old home in the middle of the night belligerent, on alcohol and drugs. He was dropped off on our doorstep by two police officers, and he wasn't very happy with my mom's cold reception. A one-sided fight ensued, and he lost his cool in a way I had never seen before. I put my ear to my door to listen to what was happening on the other side. I was too nervous to open the door; I didn't want to accidentally make eye contact with him. He was screaming and cussing at my mom, while she never even raised her voice. I don't know if she was playing it cool to push his buttons or if she was trying to lessen the chaos for me and my brother's sake.

Once he made his way into my mom's room, I cracked my door just wide enough to fit my body through and dashed down the hall to my brother's room. He opened his door just enough to let me in and then made me hide behind him. It was the first time in my life that I honestly thought my dad was going to become violent with us. We had seen him drunk on many occasions but nothing like this night. He was flinging himself wildly around my mom's room, yelling as loudly as he could. I had never feared him before, but there was something terribly wrong and frightening in him that night. My brother sensed the same and pulled a handgun out of his closet. I didn't know where the gun had come from. We had several guns in our home, but I never knew where they were or why they were there. I calmly sat behind the safety of my brother, who had barely just become a teenager, and watched as he cracked his door open and aimed his gun at our dad, who was in clear sight in our mom's room. His hand didn't shake and I found that calming. He didn't seem scared at all, which helped ease my fears. Without turning to me or taking his eyes off our dad, he whispered, "If he hits Mom I'm going to shoot him, okay?"

I said okay.

I didn't stop to think about what would happen if he pulled the trigger. I just trusted him and said okay. I didn't think about what would happen if he shot and missed or shot and hit our mom. I didn't think about what our lives would look like afterward. Would we be fatherless or motherless? Would he go to jail for murder or be set free after we explained? I didn't think about any of it. I was scared and wanted it to stop, so I just said okay. I have no idea how much time passed or how long my brother sat as still as a statue with the gun pointed at our dad, but by the grace of God my brother didn't pull the trigger. The night ended with our dad passing out and sleeping off his drunken rage. When we determined it was safe, I slipped back into my room, unnoticed by both of our parents, and went to bed. That was the night I knew that my brother would lay his life down for me at all costs.

Several days followed the day we woke up without our dad at home, and each looked the same as the one before. We woke up each morning to a child-run home. We didn't dare tell our mom. We have known all our lives that she carried more pressure on her shoulders than most moms and wives. We omitted the truth to her on several occasions simply to spare her any more pain. The thought of calling her and letting her know that we had been abandoned in that home was pushed back deep in both of our minds. I assumed our dad was contacting her as if he were home so that she wouldn't just randomly stop by the house and find us there alone.

We made an unspoken pact to soldier through.

I wanted my mom.

I wanted my dad to come home.

It wasn't really that I missed him or wanted what he brought to our family. I just wanted a parent, an adult, someone who could drive, and I wanted my brother to be just my brother and not worry about being my guardian. I wanted God to swoop down and scoop me up. I wanted to cry out to him and beg him to come get me, but I only heard the whisper of the devil reminding me that God didn't know my name.

Aside from fear of the dark when the sun disappeared each day, we also faced the fact that food wasn't being restocked. A day or so before our dad walked out, he had cooked a huge turkey—a turkey big enough to feed an army on Thanksgiving Day. We also had a pantry stocked with Pop-Tarts, because my dad usually went the easiest route possible and Pop-Tarts were easy. They were always a staple in our home. Each morning our dad was gone, we would have a package of Pop-Tarts for breakfast. When the sun reached high noon, we would pull that turkey out of the refrigerator and set it by the pool. Every day, for two weeks, we ate a Pop-Tart for breakfast, picked at the turkey by the pool for lunch, and swam until it was too dark to be outside. We were clueless about food safety, and it never occurred to us that eating a two-week-old turkey that had sat in the sun for a few hours each day might not be good for us. We didn't turn the turkey into sandwiches or use it to top a salad. That would take too much effort on our part, and we probably didn't have the ingredients anyway. It wasn't neatly wrapped in foil or tightly sealed in Tupperware. It was on a big silver sheet pan and shoved in the refrigerator. It wasn't deboned and sorted; it was randomly picked from and eaten straight off the bone. We ate just enough to fill our bellies and to give us the energy needed to keep on swimming.

The Pop-Tarts seemed endless, like manna straight from heaven except wrapped in silver packaging and void of any real nourishment.

When we were in elementary school, my mom would call up to us from downstairs when it was time to wake up, and we would call down to her, "Cooked, buttered, cut." She would put some Pop-Tarts in the toaster, and when they were done she would butter them and cut them into bite-sized squares. The middle piece was always my favorite. It was the piece that didn't have any crust and was totally soaked in butter. It was the perfect piece, and I always saved it for the very last bite. It literally melted in my mouth and gave me a sense of complete satisfaction.

My brother and I didn't have the want or the patience to cook, butter, and cut our Pop-Tarts while our dad was away. We just grabbed a package, ripped it open, and ate as quickly as we could. My brother ate the crust first, then dove into the middle. Our favorite was the brown sugar and cinnamon variety, and they tasted just like their name. They were basically just a ball of sugar surrounded by cheap pastry, and we couldn't get enough of them.

Every night after a long day of swimming we crawled into our dad's bed, pretending not to be terrified, and watched TV until our eyelids felt heavy and we could no longer keep them open. I had close friends but no one knew me like my brother. No one could make me laugh and feel safe the way he could. I don't know what shows were on TV each night, but I know that my brother made me belly laugh until my stomach hurt so that when I went to sleep it was with laughter instead of fear. He knew what he was doing. He knew that he had to keep me smiling so that neither of us crumbled in sadness.

One hot afternoon while we were having a breath-holding contest, a police officer walked into our backyard. This wasn't a strange occurrence. Our house was in a private subdivision that sat in the middle of a big city. The subdivision had its own fire and police departments. It wasn't unusual for police officers to stop by for no reason and check on things. Normally they would just wave and say hi.

They hadn't made their backyard rounds since our dad went missing, and a voice inside my head was begging me to tell the officer. It screamed in my ear to let him know that we were hungry for more than just Pop-Tarts and turkey and that we were tired of swimming and of being scared. I wanted him to rescue us without telling anyone. I didn't want to get in trouble for being home alone, and I didn't want our dad to get in trouble for leaving us. I wasn't so worried about him getting in trouble but that he would get mad at us for getting him in trouble.

My fear of our dad being angry at me outweighed the pains in my stomach or the bags under my eyes, and I chose to keep my mouth shut. My brother wasn't like me; he wouldn't have the slightest need to tell the officer. He would barrel through what we were going through without help. We kept to our standard wave and polite hello, and the officer went about his way. I watched him walk off to the next yard and felt like our rescue plane had flown right over us without noticing our SOS flag.

It could have been ten days or a solid two weeks, I honestly don't know. I had lost count after a few days and tried to stop thinking about how long we had been alone. We had become numb to our routine and surrendered to the monotony of it. We almost stopped caring if he ever came home. We didn't miss him like normal kids miss their dads when they go on vacations or business trips. We simply missed the things he could provide for us as an adult, like a ride to our friend's house. It's strange that not once the entire time he was gone did we think something bad had happened to him. There was no real concern that he was in a hospital or a morgue. We knew he hadn't been abducted from his bed the morning that I noticed he was gone. He had people after him all the time, people who wanted him to pay up on his dues, but not once did we think someone had come to collect. We knew he had left us and didn't care enough to check in.

Two weeks after giving in to the fact that we had no idea when our dad would be home, the door handle twisted. Fear and relief filled me as I watched our well-dressed and well-rested dad walk through the door. His hair was combed into a perfect mullet, feathered up front and a mess of loose curls at the base of his neck. I gave him a once-over as quickly as I could, hoping he wouldn't notice. He was in his usual outfit: Levi jeans, white tennis shoes, and a polo-style shirt. I could feel the hurt brewing deep inside of me. I would have been less shocked if he was in a full-body cast or at the very least had a broken limb or stitches across his head. Knowing he was healthy and alive was both a blessing and a pain I can't describe. He was showered and shaved, and that angered me. Why, if he was healthy and able, did he leave us all alone without a single phone call to check on us or let us know where he was? Why would he not only leave us but leave us uncared for by a responsible and capable adult? Even though we were both street smart and scrappy, we were just kids. Neither one of us was brave enough to question him, or maybe we just didn't care at this point. We had become tiny adults over the past two weeks, and we almost didn't want to let him in on our adventure together. A sacred bond had formed between my brother and me, and our dad was now on the outside looking in. We pulled down the shades. He hadn't earned the right to know the details or how strong we had grown through the process. If he was concerned about how we had fared while he was gone, he didn't bother asking.

It took me a minute to notice the orange-and-white-striped bags in his hand and as soon as I did, the smell hit me. My stomach jumped for joy. His peace offering was a bag full of hamburgers and fries from our favorite fast-food burger joint. The orange-and-white-striped Styrofoam cups held ice-cold soda, and my mouth began to water before I could get the straw to my lips. I forced myself to stop before the cup was empty, so I would have something left to complement my cheeseburger. By the time we had the burgers unwrapped we had almost forgotten that we had just spent two weeks eating only Pop-Tarts and a weeks-old turkey. The comfort of our favorite burgers and fries almost immediately erased the anger from his abandonment. It's pretty sad that fast food made up for what we had lost. As my brother held his fully loaded cheeseburger up, about to take a bite, our Great Dane walked by, snatched it out of his hand, and had it completely swallowed before we could even react. I froze, not knowing if I should laugh or scream at the dog.

It was then that my fifteen-year-old brother began to cry. My brother, who didn't shed a tear at the news of our parents' divorce, began to cry over the stolen hamburger. My brother, who hid me behind his back while he aimed a pistol at our dad, shed tears over a fast-food meal. That's the exact moment I got him, I understood his feelings. I wanted to reach over and save his tears. I wanted to catch them in my hands, bottle them up, and preserve them so I could look at them each time I needed reassurance that we were normal kids. I wanted the courage to get up from my chair and wrap my puny arms around his strong shoulders, the shoulders that had held the burden of protecting me. But I just sat there in silence and continued to eat my food, unsure of what else I could do to make the entire scene less painful.

His tears weren't about the burger being gone. Yes, he was hungry, and he truly wanted to sink his teeth into something new and tasty after two weeks of the same nonnutritious, possibly tainted food. Those tears signified something more. They were a combination of hurt for being left, anger for being handed the responsibility of a thirteen-year-old little girl, fear for what was to come, and sadness for what we had been through. The tears were for himself and for me; not a single tear that rolled off his face and slammed onto the tile floor was for our father. With a completely broken heart I watched my brother shed angry tears that day, and I will never forget each and every one that wet his cheeks.

We've whispered to each other about those days many times over the years. We call them the Turkey-Pop-Tart-Sandwich days. Sometimes we can joke about them with our families, but there are other times we talk in private. I've called him many times to ask if the story is true. Did it really happen or did I make it up in my head? Sometimes it doesn't feel real, and I need verification from the only other person that gets my confusion. It wasn't a true physical suffering on our part; we didn't starve and we certainly weren't malnourished. I've seen what neglect and child endangerment look like, and I have a hard time believing that's what happened to us. We were in a six-bedroom home that was spotless and, for the most part, extremely safe. We had food, showers, and each other. I don't think I can call it abuse. We weren't physically hurt or verbally chopped down. The suffering we felt was silent, it was an emptying of our souls. It was abandonment that didn't look like what you expect abandonment to look like. We giggled and played while we were left alone. Can that really be abuse? We didn't discuss it with each other as we went through it. For each other's sake, we pretended it was normal and okay, like any other summer day we'd had before. My brother put on a brave face because that's what you do for your little sister. I pretended not to be scared because that's what you do for your big brother.

We never asked where he had been, we knew better. We knew we wouldn't get the truth, and a lie wouldn't have satisfied us. We hadn't believed a word that came out of his mouth for years before this.

I actually wanted to thank him for leaving us all alone, so desperate that for the first time in my life I had no other choice but to turn my face to my other Father. Every night, after the TV turned to a scrambled mess of black and white, I would pray. For the first time, I wholeheartedly prayed to the Father I didn't know and who I wasn't sure knew me. Desperation brought me to his feet. I didn't know if he was real or if he cared that I was begging for him to notice me. While I can't say for sure that my prayers were answered the way I had hoped, I can say for sure that God formed a bond between me and my brother those two weeks that would save my heart on many levels for years to come. And for that I will forever be grateful for the Turkey-Pop-Tart-Sandwich days.

# FOUR

# What Can Wash Away
# My Sins

After the Turkey-Pop-Tart summer, my parents moved back in together and had an off-and-on relationship. Sometimes my dad was home, and other times he lived somewhere else. I don't think there was ever a solid relationship between him and my mom after that summer, but my mom tried over and over for the sake of her family. He was still present, for the most part, when I started high school and for a year or two into it. As I grew into my teen years, his lies and manipulation became a bigger game for us to play. Even though time after time he let me down and hurt me, I still hoped that he was going to miraculously change into this amazing father. I knew better than to trust his lies—I knew deep inside that every word was false—but I pretended to believe them.

One Friday afternoon, the promise of a fun-filled weekend with my cousins was all I could think about. I watched the clock slowly tick, second by second, as I sat in my last class waiting for the bell to release us from school for a couple of days. I turned my body to face the door, making sure I would have a clean break at the sound of the bell. I had ants in my pants and could hardly contain myself in the chair.

*Set me free! Let me go!*

I couldn't stand school. I no longer fit in despite my circle of friends and cheerleader status. In my head, I was different. They thought they knew me, but they were so far off it almost made me sad that I had them fooled with my lies. If they knew what secrets hid behind my smile, they wouldn't really be my friends. I just wanted out of there. I wanted to be with my cousins, the ones who got the real me.

At the sound of the bell I bolted from my seat and headed straight for the door, not even stopping at my locker to get what I needed or put away what I didn't. My dad was waiting for me outside, and we were headed straight to the lake. Even though our relationship had taken many twists and turns, I still trusted him enough to be his accomplice. He had blurred the line between friend and father, and I no longer cared enough to sort it out. I used him and he used me. The only time I communicated with him was when I wanted something he could get, and he would come around acting like a dad when he wanted to make an impression on people. We had settled on that kind of relationship without speaking about it.

I still craved a real father. I craved a dad that made me feel special and valued, but I settled for what I had. He wasn't ever going to be my knight in shining armor. He wasn't even part of the backup plan anymore. But he came around every so often and when he did, I grasped at the chance to feel like he loved me.

As I burst out the front doors of school, I could see my car waiting for me at the curb. My dad had given me a 1990 jet-black Eagle Talon, and I truly thought it was mine. My mom told me over and over not to get attached to it and that it wouldn't be mine for long, but in my heart I wanted to believe that this time it was for real, that my dad had legally purchased it for me. He had a habit of giving us stolen cars and had been stealing them long before I had a license. Even though I knew he didn't get the cars the way other people did, I didn't realize they were stolen until I was well into adulthood. Sometimes he drove them straight off the lot for a test drive or "borrowed" cars from his friends and handed us the keys like the car was a gift. By this time we had been given more stolen cars than I could count, but each time we chose to believe it was real.

I almost ran to the car, knowing my dad was in the driver seat waiting for our weekend trip. I yanked the door open as fast as I could and flew into the passenger seat, only to see my dad's best friend with his hands on the steering wheel.

"Where's my dad?"

"I don't know. He told me to come get you and take you to the lake."

"Why?"

"I don't know, but he said for you to stay with me."

A normal, smart teenage girl would have gotten out of the car, but I stayed. This wasn't the first time this man had picked me up from school. It had actually become normal. My dad would send him to pull me out of school, and he would take me to lunch for no reason. He had built some sort of trust with me, and I went along with his and my dad's game.

Despite what I knew about this man, I had zero fear of him. He wasn't good. He wasn't someone you drop your kids off with and he wasn't someone you trusted, especially with your daughter. He was a crook, just like my dad, and maybe that's what drew me to him. Maybe that's why I had some sort of weird twisted trust in him. He was a bad boy with a scar down his face and was built in a way that intimidated those around him. He didn't back down from anything. He was estranged from his family because even they could see that having him around was unhealthy. But I saw him differently. He was kind to me. He didn't treat me like a child, and I felt oddly protected when I was with him. He was close to ten years older than I, but our strange friendship brought us to the same level. We had completely normal conversations and laughed like old friends. When he took me out of school for lunch, we'd go straight to lunch, enjoy the hour or so, and then he'd take me right back. Nothing more. We were friends.

In addition to sending this man to pick me up from school and take me to lunch on several occasions, my dad also started filling my purse with little blue pills. He would hand them over to me by the handful. They were given to help me with anxiety—which I didn't even have. My dad created imaginary anxiety in my life and prescribed Xanax as the fix. He was suddenly my doctor and pharmacist. He told me I could take one whenever I wanted or needed it. He said it would make me less nervous and less stressed. I was not either of the two but took the pills anyway. I just believed him. I believed that he knew what was best for me and that somehow taking these pills would make me better or make my life easier to deal with. I don't know where they came from or why he felt the need to give them to me but I took them, often. They would put me into a mild coma on a daily basis, and my grades began to suffer along with my friendships. He had convinced me that I needed the meds and that they would help, but, like everything else he touched, they made me sick and dependent.

The day that my dad sent his friend to pick me up after school, I should have gotten out of the car and asked someone else for a ride home. Instead, I closed the door and watched him put the car in first gear. It was more important to get to the lake than it was to do the right thing. In the back of my head I wondered how mad my mom was going to be when she found out this man had driven me to the lake. The need to get to the lake outweighed the fear of her anger. I reached in my purse and grabbed a little blue pill, knowing it would make me not care.

The hour drive was completely uneventful. We were friends and joked and talked like we were in the same grade at school and had known each other forever. Despite what everyone thought about him and the kind of man I knew he truly was, I liked him. We had a comfortable friendship that never crossed any inappropriate line. I was neither impressed by him nor put off by him. He was a friend, and even though from the outside looking in it may have seemed alarming, it wasn't. I knew he was a criminal, but that lifestyle had always been a part of my life. It wasn't strange to me; it was normal. I had already learned the ins and outs of it: I knew what I could ask and what I couldn't; I knew when to act like an adult and when to be a kid. I was wise beyond my years. My dad took me to a bar for the first time when I was thirteen years old. It was on a school night but that didn't matter. It would be the first of many nights that I would sit in a booth at a bar and watch my dad get drunk. Then I'd get in the passenger seat of his car, too young to drive myself, and go home in time to get ready for school. There was a bar right off the highway called The Horned Toad. It was attached to a hotel and had become a hot spot for my dad. I don't know why he took me with him instead of letting me sleep. Maybe I was bait because the women in the bar flocked to me. While I sipped my Dr Pepper, they sat next to me and giggled at how cute I was. I was wise beyond their years, and I knew their game even when they didn't. I knew buttering me up was an easy way to get to my dad, who was always the most handsome guy in the room and who they thought had a loaded bank account. I played along because it was nicer than laughing in their faces.

While sitting in that dingy bar, I wondered if I was like them in God's eyes. Did he consider us the same? Did he know their names and not mine, or did he not know any of us? If there was a God, as I had heard so many people say there was, why was he putting me in the corner booth of that bar? I strained to hear God's voice over the loud lounge band but only heard the laugh of Satan reminding me that I was his.

As my dad's friend and I pulled into an empty spot in the yard of the lake house I could see my family smile at our arrival. The windows were tinted, and they only knew who was there because of the car; they didn't yet know who held the keys. They assumed my dad and I would emerge from the car. I soaked the scene in before the car stopped. My aunts, uncles, and cousins were sprawled out over the property. Some were in lawn chairs and some were on the porch, some were in the boat and some were swimming in the lake. I wanted to make a mad dash to the bedroom upstairs so I could change into my bathing suit and jump in the perfectly smooth water. I wanted to be dripping with lake water all weekend long and get so kissed by the sun it would hurt to sleep. The lake has always been my favorite place to be. It's carefree, and time moves so slowly that the days seem to last forever.

I only made it a few steps from the car when a few of my aunts and uncles realized whom I was with.

"What's he doing here?"

"Dad told him to bring me."

"He can't stay here."

My trip to the lake didn't last as long as I thought it would. Everything in me wanted to stay, and the part of me that made good decisions begged the other part of me not to get back in the car. But he insisted I stay with him like my dad had said, and against my better judgment I got back in the passenger seat and shut the door. I sat in silence while secretly wishing someone on the other side would open it up and demand that I get out. I waited for someone to open that door and grab me.

He started the car, put it in drive, and drove out of the driveway. I turned and watched out the back window as the lake got smaller and smaller and then was completely out of sight.

It's not their fault.

I was a hard teenager to deal with. I thought I was smarter than everyone else, and I did what I wanted regardless of the consequences I was sure would follow. The adults looking back at me through the rear window were probably exhausted by me at this point. They didn't have the fight in them that they knew I had in me. It was easier to just let me do what I wanted.

As we drove off, he was laughing at my family because he had won. The prize was sitting next to him, and he was driving away with it. The pit of my stomach ached, not out of fear of him but out of fear for the trouble I was going to be in. If I had stayed I would have been in trouble with my dad, but I knew that leaving meant I would be in trouble with everyone else in my life. As usual, my need to gain approval from my dad outweighed everything else. It was my choice to get back in the car, but it was my dad's fault I was there in the first place. Not a single other person was to blame for where I was that day.

Halfway back home we pulled into the only gas station on the highway. He grabbed a few quarters and headed to the pay phone to place our dinner order at my favorite Chinese restaurant. He made a few more phone calls, but none were to my dad letting him know what had happened. For the time being, he was going to keep it a secret, delaying whatever ramifications we each would face.

We picked up our to-go order and headed to his apartment. The sun had already tucked itself in for the night, and by the time we reached his doorstep the only light was from the moon and the streetlight on the corner. I could see the door to my high school from his front porch and tried to wish myself back into the desk seat I had been so desperate to escape only hours before. I wasn't scared of being alone with him; I still had absolutely no fear of him. But I ached for my family and to be one of the normal ones diving into the fresh lake water. I knew I was in trouble for leaving, and I didn't want to face any of it.

We sat down across from each other at his black-lacquer, glass-top table and made small talk while we ate our meals. By the time we finished it was late, and neither of us wanted to do anything but sleep. He offered his bed and I accepted, thinking he would take the couch. I crawled on top of the blanket and tried to get comfortable. He lay down on the other side, skipping the couch altogether. It didn't bother me; he never gave me cause for concern. I felt no fear or discomfort. I was tired and just wanted to sleep off the entire day and somehow prepare myself for what I would face the next. I turned my back toward him and shut my eyes, hoping to fall into a deep sleep.

I felt safe and comfortable and could have easily fallen asleep, right up to the moment when his warm, strong hand gripped the back of my neck. In that moment I was unable to move, completely consumed with fear. For the first time since becoming friends with him, he disrespected me and treated me like nothing more than a piece of trash. He spent the next several minutes sinning against me as I lay paralyzed with fear. I didn't fight or scream. I didn't say no or yell for him to stop. I froze and wondered what kind of trouble I was truly in.

There was no violence and there was no affection. When it was over he pulled the blanket out from under me like a magician pulling the tablecloth out from under a perfectly set table. His silence was deafening, and I wondered if he could hear the vibrations of my shaking body. He tossed the blanket in the laundry room and flopped back down on the bed beside me. Without a single word he fell asleep. For the second time that night I turned my body away from him, but this time was out of fear. I could hear his heavy breathing, in and out, while I lay there staring at the wall, completely devastated at what he had just done to me. My body felt no pain, but my soul had just been destroyed.

The phone began ringing before the sun made its appearance, and I knew it was my dad looking for me. I felt a nudge on my back.

"Get out of here."

I had been lying in the same position for hours waiting for this man to give me permission to leave. I quietly got out of bed, grabbed the keys to the car, and left his apartment. My heart was racing, and I did my best not to leave skid marks in the parking lot from driving out of the complex as quickly as I could. I was more scared in that moment than I was when I felt his hand on the back of my neck. I knew I was in trouble for putting myself in that position. I should have stayed at the lake with my family. I had made an extremely poor decision that cost me more than I had ever bargained for. My mom would be crushed. This would kill her. My brother would kill him, not backing down, like the day he pointed the gun at our dad. I feared they would all disown me for being so stupid and now so dirty.

The only place I knew to go was my friend's house. She knew me well and accepted me despite it. By the time I reached her front door I had made my mind up. I would lie. I was good at lying. I had learned from the best. What had happened behind the door of the apartment would stay locked inside me forever.

When she opened the door and let me in I could hear her phone ringing.

"It's your dad."

I didn't even say hello. I picked up the receiver, and by the time it reached my ear I could hear him yelling. He demanded I meet him immediately. I had no idea what he knew. The actions of his best friend the night before had everything in me completely twisted.

I pulled into the parking lot of our favorite fast-food BBQ restaurant. The complex right behind it was where my mom had lived in a one-bedroom apartment many years before. I wondered how differently things would have turned out if my brother and I had made the choice to live with her. My stomach had never hurt this way before. I was gagging from extreme nausea and wanted to vomit. My neck throbbed with each beat of my heart. I wanted nothing more than to sit there and sob. Instead, I sat up straight and took a deep breath. I slowly got out of my car, moving as though I was caught in quicksand, and reluctantly got into the passenger side of the car my dad was driving.

There were only two sentences spoken in that car.

"If you ever tell your mother what happened, I will make your life a living hell. Get out."

I was speechless. I had thought I was going to get into trouble for leaving the lake and for what had happened the night before. I had thought my dad would be hurt and sad for me and worried about my well-being. But in just two sentences he let me know his true feelings. He was more concerned with my mom finding out and getting into trouble himself than he was about me.

His words were completely unnecessary. He had already made my life a living hell. How much more damage could he do than what he had done? He put that man in my life. He made me trust him. He had him pick me up from school and told me to go with him over and over. He had filled my purse with little blue pills to make me more easygoing. Maybe choosing to leave the lake was my fault, but my dad made the choice to hand me over to this man as if I was nothing more than a piece of garbage. I was the child and he was the parent. He was supposed to protect me from this kind of evil, not feed me to it. I exited my dad's car a completely different person from when I got in. The fight was on. I left the sad little girl behind and got back in my car an angry woman. Fear of breaking my mother's heart kept me silent. Fear of my dad making good on his words kept me from telling the truth about the details of that night. The voices in my head were different from the one now coming out of my mouth. Lying became easier, almost habitual. I began to enjoy self-destruction and was proud of the fact that I was rougher than most girls. I still longed for my dad to save the day, but I was coming to terms with the fact that he was the one I needed saving from.

I lived my life in fear of being found out. I told only a very few people in my little world. I didn't understand that it wasn't my fault. I didn't understand that at the age of sixteen and in the situation my dad had placed me, I wasn't capable of making the right choice or giving consent. I was a child. My dad's friend was an adult. He made an adult decision that night that I wasn't capable of making or fighting. But fear kept me quiet. I was terrified of others learning the truth. I feared being in trouble. I feared hurting anyone who loved me. I feared looking dirty. I feared my dad hating me. I feared his friend's wrath. So I stayed quiet, at least on the outside. On the inside, however, everything was loud and clear. I singlehandedly destroyed every male relationship I had from that point on. I didn't want the men in my life to know I wasn't good enough for them, so I would, at all cost, tear down every relationship that had even a hint of getting close enough to see the truth.

# FIVE

# Invisible Girl

It had been a year since my dad sat in his car and verbally confirmed that I held very little worth in his eyes. His last words to me face-to-face still burned a hole in my heart. Behind my smile and humor I hid a very dark secret. Faking things had become easy, and being part of the cheerleading squad gave me an outlet to pretend to be something I wasn't.

I blended in. I tied my hair up into a ponytail and clipped on a bright red-and-white bow and instantly became one of them. Add a uniform and a little makeup and you almost couldn't tell us apart. I worked hard to be the loudest and the best because I could no longer stand defeat. When I watched one of the other girls accomplish a goal, I planned how I would top it. They were all kind and good, so I pretended to be too.

Our school was built on traditions. I attended the same high school my parents had attended and held the same position as cheerleader that my mom had. On the surface

I was following in her footsteps, but deep down I was dark and she was light. When I dug through pictures and found her in her cheer uniform with the same patch on her jacket that I had on mine, her smile jumped right off the photo and lit up the room. So I practiced her smile in hopes that I would light up the room the same way she had at my age. I hid behind her smile, and it worked. She was my biggest fan. She sat in the stands and cheered the loudest at every event. She stood up for me and supported me even when I was in the wrong. I secretly wished I was more like her and less like me.

My bright red uniform and big bow made me feel like I fit somewhere. When people looked at me, they saw me the same way they saw the other girls. Fitting in made me feel like my deep wounds were invisible. I learned to love it. I was happy when I was with my cheerleading team. They made me feel accepted and normal.

My favorite tradition was packing up one of the girl's family vans and driving several hours to attend cheer camp each summer. We stuffed our matching duffel bags full of coordinating uniforms, shirts, shorts, and bows. Each of us had a personalized pillowcase, and we took bags and bags of snacks to last us all week. It always felt like a big vacation to me. I knew we had hard work and sweaty days ahead, but it was a break from our daily routines with only one thing to think about—winning cheer camp.

We put in hard work each year, and each year we came home with a trophy. I absolutely loved the feeling of winning and being a team and working together.

While we worked hard at camp, we found ways to play even harder. As teenagers, it was equally as important to goof off as it was to win, and we were good at goofing off. We spent almost an hour every day of camp completely abandoning any responsibility and just acting like kids. Two of my closest girlfriends and I would pack ourselves onto a small twin bed during lunch break and sing songs together like we were a trio in a concert. We would put our tongues on the roof of our mouths and sing Reba McEntire's "The Greatest Man I Never Knew" in our goofiest voices and laugh until tears filled our eyes. They were my girls, my go-to people, with whom I could either tell jokes until we couldn't breathe from laughter or cry until our makeup ran onto our shirts. They knew my broken pieces and wide-open cracks, but they stayed and made the best of wherever we were.

Another tradition rooted deep in our school was the Spring Show. Our entire spirit team would gather for two evenings and perform for our friends and family. It was a rite of passage for all of us and something we looked forward to the moment we entered high school. The dance team prepared their best routines and the cheerleaders performed their toughest stunts. It was a night of showing off our greatest accomplishments from the year and cheering on each other's victories. Every participant anticipated the event with excitement all year long. Everyone except me.

I dreaded it.

Part of the tradition was for the senior girls to dress up in their best dresses and dance with their dads to "Daddy's

Little Girl." It was such a beautiful dance and an extremely special moment for most of the girls. There were probably others like me who didn't have a dad to dance with or whose dad refused to show, but it's not something we talked about. As the girls giggled with excitement over dancing with their dads, I got knots in my stomach.

I had known this day was coming for four years. I knew that one day I'd be a senior and would have to face the father-daughter dance. My dad knew it was coming too, and since I had stopped answering his phone calls, he started sending me letters asking when the dance was. He assumed I wouldn't have the courage to tell him no and he was right. I didn't have the courage to tell him that I didn't want to dance with him, so I ignored him. I avoided his phone calls and never replied to his letters. I wanted him to just go away; I wanted to pretend that it wasn't happening this year. It would hurt less to show up to the dance alone than to have my father accept my rejection and not fight to be with me. After all that had happened, I still wanted him by my side, but he had failed to earn that spot.

One day I picked up the phone without checking caller ID and found my dad on the other end. I could tell by the tone of his voice that he felt victorious. He had me cornered and we both knew it. The mere mention of the dance made me want to faint, and I panicked over telling him he wasn't invited. So I lied. It's his fault. He made me a liar. He helped me master the skill of lying long before I knew it was wrong. He taught me how to lie in the second grade when he declared a Snell Holiday and allowed me to skip school for a family emergency that didn't exist. He taught me this skill and I now was going to use it against him.

I told him our school wasn't having the dance this year. I tried to make him believe that after several years of tradition, they randomly decided not to have the dance my senior year. But you can't con a con man. I knew he didn't believe me, but I kept it up anyway.

I didn't want to dance with my dad, but I also hadn't wanted to be the only senior girl forced to sit on the sidelines. My mom had been dating her boyfriend for a very short time, and desperation for a father figure brought me to him. Completely humiliated by not having a partner for the father-daughter dance, I asked him if he would be willing to dance with me. He wouldn't have to pretend he was my dad; everyone knew who my real dad was and that he was no longer a part of my life. I just needed someone to stand in for him.

The man with two left feet and zero rhythm agreed to fill the gap my dad was leaving. I was relieved to know I wouldn't be left out of the traditional dance, but there was no relief in the fact that I wouldn't be dancing with my dad. I knew there would be whispers, and I knew there would be a man with a crushed heart.

In the days leading up to the show we had several practices, some with the dads and some without. Mine were always without. My mom's boyfriend wasn't there for a single practice, not because he didn't want to be but because he wasn't able to make it. Whatever the reason, it left me standing alone. The senior girls would line up on one side and all the dads would line up across from us, each face-to-face with his daughter. I was face-to-face with an empty spot. Seeing all the dads beam with pride as they stood across from their little girls made it that much more obvious. It's a choice I had made for myself, but it made me feel invisible. I could easily have had my dad fill that space, but it hurt less to be alone than to have him fake being a super dad. He would have acted like Dad of the Year, and every single person in that room would have known better. I chose the blank space.

No one at practice said anything. No one asked where my dad was. The other senior girls had been in my life long enough to know why the spot across from me was empty. Because I had built a wall around me and learned to fake a smile so well, they didn't know how embarrassed I was or how worthless I felt or how jealous I was of each of them. They thought I was fine because that's what I always told them.

I smiled along with the others girls while I danced with one of the younger girls who stood in for my dad during practice. We giggled because it was funny to see me with another kid while all the girls were with their dads. I giggled because it was better than crying.

We performed the Spring Show two nights in a row. It was the same performance each night but two nights gave parents and family the opportunity to make it to one of them. Two nights gave opportunity to display my rejection twice. On the first night all the senior girls gathered in the dressing room and got ready for the grand finale, the father-daughter dance. It was the last event each night and the moment parents and daughters were most excited about. The girls were giddy. I watched them carefully get ready, making sure each hair was in place and ironing out any wrinkles in their dresses. Their jewelry was sparkling, and their smiles were bright. I was truly happy for them. I didn't wish what was in my heart on any of them. But I was incredibly jealous. I wished I was as excited about the dance as they were. I wanted to have my best jewelry rolled up in a special pouch waiting to be revealed around my neck. I wanted my dad to be outside the door with sweaty hands, eagerly anticipating our dance together. I carelessly threw on my old prom dress, pulled my ponytail out, and let my hair fall where it may. Without even touching up my makeup, I decided I was ready.

It was almost time for the dance. All the other performances were just about wrapped up and there was still no sign of my mother's boyfriend. He hadn't made it to a practice, and I began to doubt that he was going to show up to the big night.

As the other girls made their way backstage, I made my way outside. One of the girls who had sung silly songs with me at cheer camp walked outside with me in the hopes that she would be there to see my knight in shining armor finally arrive. We stood together watching the road, and every once in a while she would give me a knowing smile, trying to silently tell me everything was okay. After what seemed like hours, I told her to leave and go back inside. I begged her not to talk me into going back into the auditorium; I just wanted to leave. But she just stood there with me and smiled, making me think we were more alike than we really were.

Several minutes passed and we were cutting our time very short when I saw his old blue truck turn the corner. I could always spot his truck from a long way away because it was the only one with a bright red ladder strapped to the top. My girlfriend squeezed my hand and turned to go get ready, leaving me there to greet my hero.

He slowly got out of his car because that's how he did everything, on his own time. He was apologizing for being late before I was even able to hear what he was saying. By the time he reached me his goofy grin stretched ear to ear. He was a jeans-and-T-shirt man and was late because he had trouble tying his tie. None of it mattered. I didn't care why he was late; I was just thankful he was there. I grabbed his hand and practically dragged him into the auditorium and shoved him into place, the place that had been empty for far too long.

And then we danced.

We weren't Fred and Ginger but we danced. He did his best not to step on my toes, and I did my best not to crumple into tears. Neither of us had an ounce of grace in us but neither of us cared. I wasn't alone. I wasn't the girl without a dad. We blended in perfectly, making it almost impossible for anyone to figure out which girl was dancing with a substitute dad.

I felt some sort of victory that night, and it lessened the worry of having to dance two nights in a row. My mom's boyfriend promised me to not only show up for the second dance but also to not be late.

The next day he came to my mom's house while I was packing up my outfits for the night's performances. My mom made sure his tie was tied long before he was scheduled to leave the house. I threw my old prom dress in a bag like it was a gym uniform. All I cared about was having someone to dance with; it didn't matter what either of us looked like. I wouldn't have cared if he showed up in Bermuda shorts and a flowered button-down shirt, as long as he showed.

Just as I was about to leave and head up to school, he called me into my mom's room. He was sitting on her bed with a serious look on his face, and I just knew he was going to bail on me. I said a quick prayer, to a God I had long discounted in my life, that he would make it a clean cut and that I wouldn't suffer too much. My eyes couldn't meet his, I was too scared. Just as I was about to accept that I would be alone that night, he began his speech.

"I had fun dancing with you last night but I noticed that all the other girls looked so pretty and fancy and you just looked so plain."

*Oh, God, please make him stop. Please make him just leave it at that. I can handle plain. If the worst he wants to call me is plain then I'll take it. I've been called so much worse. I've been branded worse by my own dad, I didn't need it again. Why would he do this to me right before I'm about to walk out the door to perform in front of an auditorium full of people? God, please hear me! God, my name is Candice. Do you know me? Do you know my name? If you know me please don't let this happen to me in the one moment I finally feel special.*

But he continued.

"So I bought you this."

He handed me a small black jewelry box. I looked at my mom for a clue but she just smiled back and shrugged her shoulders, letting me know she had no idea what was in the box. I took it out of his hands and slowly opened it to reveal a delicate gold necklace with a pendant that boasted three small diamonds and a single pearl.

"Now you can look fancy like the other girls."

I'm not good at accepting gifts or compliments. They both make me extremely uncomfortable, and I never know how to react. All I could say was thank you and hug his neck so tightly that there was no doubt of how grateful I was to him for showing me this kindness. Calling me plain was his setup, and I suddenly found it to be so sweet. The entire thing was out of character for him. He was a country boy with calloused hands and bad table manners. He wore jeans and old boots no matter where he went and cussed far more than the average human. But in that moment he was tender and kind. He did for me what my own father couldn't. He showed me that I was worth more than precious jewels. He gave me a token of love to wear around my neck.

When I left he shouted down the hall that now all the girls were going to be jealous of me because of my fancy necklace. I chuckled inside at how ridiculous the thought was that they would be jealous of me. He was teasing me and lightening the mood, but I know he really wanted them to be. I kind of wanted them to be jealous too. I wanted them to whisper behind my back about my beautiful necklace and how lucky I was that my stand-in dad had lavished me with this gift.

On the second night of the Spring Show I was happy, happier than I had been in a long time, and I felt precious. I felt wanted and accepted. I felt like I stood out and that maybe, just maybe, everyone in the room was secretly cheering us on.

And then we danced.

The hard truth is that even with the beautiful necklace and the generous, loving man dancing with me, the reality still stung. My mom's boyfriend showed me that I am worthy and loved, and for the rest of my life I will cherish every moment of that day. But in the corner of the auditorium lurked a sad secret.

A few days after the dance, a teacher informed me that my dad had called the school and asked when the dance was. He knew I had lied to him, but his arrogance wouldn't allow him to stay away and respect the fact that I didn't want him there. He had to see for himself. The same teacher let me know that she saw him sneak in and creep up to the balcony where no one else was seated. From way up high, in the far corner of the auditorium, my father watched me dance with the man who would soon become my stepdad, the man who would allow me to call him Dad without blinking an eye. My father watched as a strong and loving man cut in on the dance that was supposed to be his, and he watched as I gladly accepted.

After that night, contact with my dad became infrequent. I kept him at a distance without completely cutting him off. It was more comforting that way. But I made it clear that day that I no longer wanted him as a daily presence in my life and that I would prefer he kept his distance from any events I had at school.

He never could respect anyone else's wishes and continued to sneak around and watch me from a distance. I simply pretended he wasn't there.

# SIX

# What Happens in Vegas

After high school I attended college in a nearby city. I had high hopes of majoring in criminal justice and one day becoming a judge. I think it was my way of rebelling against my dad by somehow becoming what he wanted to be. He always pretended to be a lawyer, and if he hadn't been so crooked he would have excelled in law. His mind was brilliant, far too brilliant for his own good. He figured he could slide by without putting in the real work of mastering his field by getting a law degree. He knew he was smarter than most people. He could sell snow to Eskimos and convince you of anything he said. Ultimately he didn't think he needed a degree to get what he wanted, and most of the time he was right.

I wanted to prove I was better than he was. I wanted to go to school and excel in my field. In some twisted way I wanted him to be jealous of me. But I didn't handle my new freedom very well. I stunk at college. No one was holding me accountable for attending classes, and I found it hard to stay motivated. Unfortunately, I had inherited that attitude from my dad: if someone wasn't forcing me, then I wouldn't go. My dorm room was small and cozy, and it was hard to emerge from it to attend a class where I was merely a number.

I was only forty-five minutes from home but I felt alone. My girlfriend from high school roomed with me in the dorms, and as much comfort and fun as she brought to college life, I knew none of it was right for me. I was miserable. I hated being away from my cousins and felt so out of place. It seemed like everyone there was made from the same cookie cutter, and I wasn't even a cookie.

It wasn't long before I gave up and completely stopped showing up for classes. My name was on their roster, but they had no idea who I was. School became a place that made me lose myself, and before long I couldn't identify my own face. Every night I made the forty-five minute drive home to spend the night with my cousins, and every morning I drove back to school where I had taken a job at the rec center. I was no longer attending classes but continued to show up for work. For several hours a day I would pass out pool balls to the other college kids. As soon as my shift was up, I would hop back in my car and head toward the city limit sign. I was tired and miserable but lacked the courage to tell my mom I had already quit.

My mom was a dean's list type of student who busted her rear to raise two kids and attend college at the same time. Her work ethic was off the charts, and she called in sick only if she was near death.

One of my greatest fears has always been disappointing my mom. I didn't want her to see me in the same way she saw my dad, and when my actions reflected his, I hid from her. Even though she never threw him in my face or made me believe I was anything like him, I never wanted her to even have those kinds of thoughts. I knew that deep inside I had something of him in me. I knew that I had an addictive nature and that I had the ability to lie through my teeth. Those were his qualities, not hers, and I didn't want to fail her by giving in to those things. I thought I was doing her a favor by keeping secrets and not letting her see all of me.

Eventually I had to withdraw from school, because they don't let you hang around with a 0.0 average, and therefore had to leave my job too. I didn't mind. The moment I left the job and school, with my withdrawal papers in hand, I felt free. It felt like a huge weight had been lifted from my shoulders, and I went home as soon as I could. I didn't care if I looked like a failure; I just wanted to be home.

Facing my mom was what worried me the most, but if I was expecting her to completely freak out, she let me down. I bowed my head as I stood across from her in the living room and explained that I couldn't go back to school. I tried to make her understand that it made me unhappy and that it was just too much for me to be there, but I was talking to a woman who aced college while raising two young children. I know she was disappointed, but she didn't throw it in my face. Instead of telling me how much I resembled my dad— that he never followed through either—she simply told me to go that very day and find a job, because if I wasn't in school then I would be at work. Her work ethic was no match for anyone I knew, and she was more loyal to her job than anyone I had ever seen. As I stood face-to-face with the woman who flew through college and poured herself into her job, I agreed to hunt down a job of my own.

I held true to my promise that day and, after applying for a job on a dare from my cousin, I went home and proudly informed my mom that I was officially employed. I took a deep gulp and held up my new uniform. As she raised one eyebrow and stared at her daughter's new work attire, which consisted of a tight white tank top and bright orange shorts that could have been confused for underwear, she got a sly smirk on her face and said, "Good, you'll make a lot of money there." Even though I knew she was disappointed, she supported me the only way she could in that moment. Her daughter had gone from aspiring judge to Hooters girl in a matter of a few months. I imagine her heart was crushed and she worried about my future, but she did what good moms do: accepted who I was and where I was in life with a crooked smile, a raised eyebrow, and a few words of encouragement mixed with a heavy dose of sarcasm.

I promised myself out loud that I would hold a job for a short time and then head back to school to get my degree. In my head I knew I was lying and that I wouldn't step foot back in college unless it was to watch someone else graduate. As usual, I held true to the voice in my head and not the one coming out of my mouth.

I became a professional restaurant worker and mastered every job you could hold in the business. By the time I was twenty-three, I was managing a local bar that was the hot spot of the city. I wasn't where I had planned to be at twenty-three, but I was actually doing quite well and had the same work ethic my mom had. I wasn't good at taking tests or showing up for class, but I was good at working and making money. I had finally accomplished something I was proud of.

My life had made me proud and selfish. I did exactly what I wanted whenever I wanted and rarely took other people's feelings into consideration. I watched my friends graduate from college and start careers, but I found it laughable. I was young, making good money, and doing whatever I wanted. As I watched others follow the path that was expected of us, I realized that I was never going to be like them and do the normal thing. I was always going to push the envelope and fight against who someone else wanted me to be. I knew deep in my heart that I wasn't strong enough to be like them, so I pretended that I didn't want to be.

In the middle of being an independent and selfish young woman, I made another fly-by-the-seat-of-my-pants decision and ran off to Las Vegas with my boyfriend to get married.

I've never been one for weddings. They make me sweat. All I can think about is how uncomfortable the bride must be in all that lace and tulle. How is she even breathing? I always wonder if she is thinking about how uncomfortable she is instead of focusing on the joys of her wedding. The thought of having to use the restroom in one of those poufy dresses was enough to make me never want to put one on. Unlike most little girls, I never dreamed of my wedding day. I knew I wanted to get married but stressing over seating charts, flowers, and all the other details never appealed to me. I can't imagine picking out colors or going to cake tastings. I wanted to be a wife, and I prayed that my husband wouldn't mind skipping the huge wedding either.

Despite the protest from our friends and the concern from our families, we boarded a plane and headed to Sin City. He was good and smart and I was wild and free. The whirlwind excitement wiped out logical thinking on our part and two days after deciding we should get married, we were married.

In the absence of our family and friends, except for my mom and two aunts, we said "I do" and then made a beeline for the casino. It was behavior that was expected of me but to his family and friends it was shocking, and our rash decision proved hurtful.

Only a few short weeks after we got home from Vegas we found out we were pregnant. The stress and fear of becoming parents when we knew very little about being a couple, much less being pregnant, broke everything in us. Before we were able to become parents together our marriage was already falling apart. We had no idea how to navigate through what we had done and where we had ended up. We had made a selfish choice to start a marriage on quicksand, and now we were bringing a child into it. Fear consumed me. I hated myself for having the audacity to bring a child into a broken home and make it go through even an ounce of what I had as a child. For the first time my selfishness hit me, and I realized I would be responsible for the path this child would take. The weight of what I was doing to our baby was crushing.

Our marriage wasn't going to survive, but we knew that we would have to figure out a way to be good and loving parents—together.

On March 20, 2000, our daughter was born and placed in her dad's arms. The first person to hold her and look into her eyes was her dad. Seeing her in his arms took away my selfishness. In that moment, I made a promise to myself and to her that I would never let her feel desperate for her dad's love the way I had felt for mine. I wanted her dad to be her hero, her knight in shining armor. I wanted her to cling to him when she was scared and trust every word that came out of his mouth. I would make it my number one responsibility to put her relationship with him above all else and do what I could to nourish it and make it healthy. I didn't care what I would have to sacrifice; he would be the one she ran to.

Our signatures on the divorce papers and our signatures on her birth certificate dried at the same time. She had two cribs in two separate homes before she even made it out of the hospital.

We struggled to find our balance as new parents and did our best to share in the joy of raising her. I had failed her in giving her a home with both of her parents under one roof, but I would not fail her in having two parents who loved her enough to do right by her. Since we both knew how it felt to be kids of divorce, we made sure we treated each other with respect and love when she was looking. We had moments of complete despair and hurt with each other, but we became a united front for our little girl.

My daughter changed me in more ways than I ever expected. She gave me a purpose and made me a better person. She taught me how to be nice and how to make sacrifices I never wanted to make. She showed me that it's okay not to always be right. Becoming her mother freed me from the pain and hurt my dad inflicted upon me, but it didn't free me from the worthlessness I felt from not having my own dad love me enough to do right by me.

When I became a mother, my life changed. I set aside every desire I had to have him in my life or to be, on any level, his daughter. I wouldn't even allow him a peek into what I was doing or what my daughter looked like. As her mother it was my responsibility to protect her from the things I knew he was capable of, and the only way I could do that was to cut him completely out of my life. For the first time in twenty-four years, I stood up to him. With my feet firmly planted, I told him he was no longer a member of my family. He hadn't been actively involved in my life for many years, but I still fell for his act and his lies. I had allowed him to come and go when he wanted and to manipulate my feelings. Now, I played nice when we had to be at family events and allowed him to pretend he was still my dad when people were looking. However, as a mom, I was done. My little girl would never know the pain he inflicted on people. She would never know what it felt like to be kicked in the face over and over by someone you love.

My daughter was only 9 pounds, 1 ounce, but she was enough to give me the courage I needed to finally end the many years of desperately trying to force my dad to love me the way I thought I deserved.

# SEVEN

# Building a Life on Shifting Sand

I began rebuilding my life as a single mom and did my best to coparent with my ex-husband. We managed to give each other massive amounts of grace in the parenting department, and together we figured out a way to help each other balance our lives between our jobs and our little girl's separate homes.

I grew up watching my mom work hard at her job and do whatever she had to, not only just getting by but also excelling in her workplace. I tried to model her behavior and work ethic, and a few years after becoming a single mom, I was promoted to management and given a salary that would help support us both. Most of my days were spent at work and any time off was spent with my daughter. I was blessed with a huge support team, and when I was working my daughter was with either her dad or my family.

I loved every second with my daughter but I also loved my job, so there were rarely feelings of guilt for working so hard. Ultimately, I knew I was teaching her how to work hard and cherish each moment at the same time. Since I had already been working for the company for almost ten years, most of the people there were like my second family. For the first time in a long time I felt comfortable and secure. I felt good about where I was in life. For the first time in a long time, I didn't feel that there was something missing.

A few months into a new management role, I was told we were getting a new manager from a neighboring city and that he would be my boss. I determined right then, before he even stepped foot in the restaurant, not to like him. All I knew was that he had been in a manager's position longer than I had, by several years, and that he was much younger than I. I pictured some young punk coming in and bossing everyone around as though he'd been here for years, and I decided that wasn't going to happen. The poor guy was a marked man before he even had a chance to say hello.

On his first day, I put on my best tough-girl attitude and headed into work. Trying not to appear obvious, I looked around for him. I needed to size him up before he saw me. I needed to have the upper hand. I wouldn't be caught off guard.

I rounded a corner and there he was. He was helping our bartender stock shelves, and he glanced up as I walked by. A simple "Hi" was all he would get from me; he would have to earn the rest.

"Hi, I'm Brandon."

"Hey."

"I really like your hair."

"Um, thanks."

*What?*

*Is he serious?*

I really like your hair? That was his ice-breaking line? If there was something I wasn't prepared for it was the new guy opening with a hair compliment.

I stayed away from him for as long as I could. I avoided being caught in the office with him and never invited him to eat with me after our shifts. We were simply coworkers, and I was comfortable leaving it at that.

But he had other plans. He began scheduling us to work together as often as possible. Every time I got my schedule I could see that his and mine were almost identical. Secretly I thought it was kind of cute but never showed an ounce of interest in him. I had made a promise to myself that I wasn't going to become his friend or even like him.

Our days always turned into nights as we closed the restaurant and sent the staff home, leaving just the two of us to finish up paperwork, set the alarm, and lock up the building, most nights walking out the door long after midnight. On those nights that we closed together he took his time, slowly going through each task we needed to accomplish before we left. And we started to talk. We talked about everything in our lives. We spent hours alone forming a deep friendship I never saw coming. We talked about our daughters and what we wanted for their lives and what we wished our futures looked like. We talked about where we had come from and how we ended up where we were now. Our lives had uncommon similarities that most people don't have in their lives. There was no denying that we understood each other and could relate to everything the other had been through.

One night, in the middle of one of our talks, he told me that he just wanted a family. He wanted a family to go home to each night after work. He wanted a wife and family to share dinner with and kiss goodnight. He wanted normalcy and routine, and I found that to be his most endearing quality. I couldn't help but smile at this man who was opening himself up to me. He was gentle and kind, and in my head I thought how lucky the woman was who would get to be his bride. I was almost jealous of this future wife. I made a wish to find someone who wanted what he wanted. I wished for a husband with a heart like the man who was standing in front of me. The guy I had decided not to like before I even met him was suddenly becoming one of my strongest confidants and an example of a man I needed in my life.

After sitting in the office many nights confessing our life's desires, we started hanging out in the front of the restaurant once everyone had cleared out. We cranked up the radio, set to our favorite country station, and we danced. I don't recall how it started or how he asked, but he would take my hand in his and we would two-step around the restaurant as if we were the only two people in the world. The only light that entered the building was from the street lights outside and the occasional headlights from passing cars. We both smelled like the deep fryer in the kitchen and we were covered in food stains, but neither of us cared.

For the first time in years, I felt completely safe and comfortable just being me, the real me. He didn't care about where I had been or what I had done. He just cared about being with me.

After one long night of sharing many other details of our lives, he confessed that he had fallen in love with me. Even though I had carefully built a wall around my heart, he had somehow gained my trust and love. He had found his way in.

As careful as I had been about letting him into my life, once he was, there was no stopping us. Only a few months later we were standing in front of the justice of the peace saying our vows.

We got married on a Thursday. It was easy to agree on because we both had the day off and knew the courthouse wouldn't be busy. The details of a wedding didn't concern either of us; we just wanted to seal our marriage and get on with our life together. We were out of pocket sixty dollars, which included parking and lunch at a local restaurant. My mom and my brother's wife met us at the courthouse to witness the big event, and my daughter skipped school to watch her mom get married. It was a free-for-all, and everyone showed up in whatever was most comfortable. My daughter chose a pink, glittery Mrs.-Santa-style dress with white fur-lined cuffs and matching Santa hat. It was a hot Texas day in mid-March but that didn't matter to her. She dressed in what she thought was her most beautiful outfit, and we didn't stop her. There was no outside pressure or need to look a certain way, have matching outfits, wear a poufy dress, or have a perfectly decorated cake; we just enjoyed becoming Mr. and Mrs. Curry.

The lack of stress that day was a far cry from what we would face in our marriage. Neither of us was prepared for what was to come, and before we even made it through the year, we found ourselves struggling to catch our breath. We had failed miserably to build our life on a sturdy foundation. We thought we could build as we went, but we failed to lay the groundwork for success. We both came from families of divorce. My entire life I had bailed on the hard stuff without considering the rewards that might come from the sacrifices. I was a my-way-or-the-highway type of girl and when things went south, I ran. I never knew that weathering the storm was what often brought the rainbows.

**Rescue Me**

We knew we were pregnant before we said I do, and only a week after our quick nuptials we headed to our first doctor's appointment. We had randomly picked a doctor with a few recommendations from our friends because my regular doctor couldn't fit me in for several weeks. Reluctantly we headed to a new and unknown office to learn when the baby was due. There was no fear about the pregnancy; we had both agreed that we wanted more children. We each had a daughter from previous marriages and couldn't wait to add to our blended family. The pregnancy wasn't a surprise and even though we didn't have the perfect plan, it was our plan and what we wanted.

We filled out several forms and were led back to the sonogram room where we eagerly waited to get a glimpse of our baby's heartbeat. Brandon held my hand in support, and I tried to give him a comforting smile through my own nervousness. The sonographer squeezed the cold blue gel onto the machine and gently placed it on my stomach. I held my breath. While both of our eyes were glued to the screen, she softly moved the probe over my stomach and searched for the baby's faint heartbeat. We waited. We waited some more, until she moved the screen out of our view and excused herself from the room to get the doctor.

This wasn't the first time in a room like this for either of us, and we both immediately knew that something wasn't right. Neither of us was brave enough to speak the first word and acknowledge what was going on. So we sat in silence and waited. Everything about the room was cold, from the actual temperature to the bareness of the room. She left the lights off, and the darkness gave way to despair. The absence of light created a deep place to think hard thoughts.

The sonographer came back in accompanied by the doctor and a nurse. After giving us polite introductions, they began to search my belly once more. Slowly and methodically the doctor covered every inch in me that could possibly hold the beating heart of our child. Once again they found no heartbeat and asked me to please get dressed and meet the doctor in his office.

As I carefully stepped down from where I had been lying, the ice-cold floor came as a shock. I hadn't remembered it being that cold. I felt more fragile than when we had made our way back to the room. I didn't want to move too fast and somehow hurt the child any more than I had already.

Everything seemed like it was about to fall apart, and the slower I got dressed the more time it bought us before our world crumbled.

Brandon sat in silence. Nothing he could say was going to ease the tension and sadness we were feeling. In an effort to spare my feelings for just a few more minutes, he pretended like everything was okay. Out of the corner of my eye I saw him sending a text, and I knew he was preparing our family for my phone calls or lack thereof. Once I was dressed he sweetly took my hand and guided me down the hall to the doctor's office. What had seemed like a short walk just minutes before had now become a never-ending hall. We reached the door to his office, and he invited us to come in and sit down. The first sentence out of his mouth was that we were miscarrying twins. After that I heard nothing but a dull vibration in my ears rather than words. I mentally checked out and hoped Brandon was listening. From what the doctor could tell, one of the twins had not formed correctly and was unable to survive. The other twin had lived only a week or so longer, then lost its heartbeat along with its sibling.

I didn't care about details and just wanted him to let us leave. I needed to kick and scream, and I did my best to keep the tears from waterfalling down my face.

The receptionist scheduled another appointment exactly one week later and gave us some instructions to follow prior to arriving.

They sent me home with a womb that had failed to sustain the life of two babies and an appointment to have them removed. Even though I knew my husband's heart was equally crushed, my self-pity was overwhelming and I couldn't help him through his pain. I needed to go home and sleep for a week and not face anything else the world had for me. I called in sick to work, turned my phone off, and pulled the sheets over my head. The crying never stopped, and Brandon did his best to comfort me. He worked his shifts at the restaurant and covered mine, pulling double duty to save me from having to see anyone. The loss of a child was overwhelming, but the loss of two and the loss of the chance at twins was more than I could bear. I didn't want to hear anyone's attempt at words of comfort. I just wanted to sit still for seven full days, completely by myself.

In those seven days I pleaded with God, the God I had heard everyone speak so lovingly about, the God I was told was good and helpful—the God that clearly either didn't know me or didn't exist. I only ever spoke to him out of desperation, not truly believing that my words would reach anywhere. If he was listening, he had heard me only in times of need. I pretended to believe in him when I thought he could help me. I didn't give him thanks for any of the blessings he had given me, and I never prayed just to pray. I had never prayed out of obedience; I always had a motive. I never even thought to speak to him unless I was worried or needed him to rescue me. I spent seven straight days begging him to forgive me, making promises to him that I knew I wouldn't keep. If ever I wanted him to know my name, to truly know who I was, it was now. I knew that he wasn't happy with the life I had been living but begged him not to hold it against these babies. I promised to change, and this time I didn't cross my fingers. I didn't live a life that deserved to be blessed with such abundance, but I held out hope that God had a better plan than the one I had been living.

We made it through the week and prepared ourselves for the appointment where they would finalize the loss of our children. Our friends and family offered what they could and asked if we needed anything. Our only request was that someone take care of our oldest daughter, so she wouldn't know our sadness and it wouldn't interrupt her sweet and innocent world. We hadn't told her that we were pregnant but had told her that we were going to try for a baby. She had bowed her head and prayed, "God, please put a baby in Mommy's tummy."

When we arrived at our appointment they led us down the same hall we had gone down the week before. Our first trip down the hall had been full of hope and excitement. Our second trip was full of sadness and loss. I stepped behind the curtain and changed into the paper-like gown and made my way onto the table, so they could once again put a picture on the screen of my failed attempt at carrying life. I was angry at the doctor for making us go through another sonogram and just wanted to get it all over with. My husband sat as close as he could but knew I wasn't in the mood to be coddled or touched. He sat still and silent with his eyes once again fixed on the screen. I stared at the wall without so much as a glance at it.

The tech was different from the one we had the week before, and she did her best to keep the appointment as routine as any other pregnancy appointment. She was cheery and bright, but it didn't change anything for me or Brandon. Once again the cold gel hit my belly and we held our breath just to make it through what we already knew.

After a minute or so I heard a familiar noise, the swishing of a tiny heartbeat growing inside of me. I had heard it before with my daughter and nothing can ever erase that sound from a mom's memory. I swung my head toward my husband and could see by the look on his face that he knew the sound too.

There was a heartbeat.

"Is that a heartbeat?"

"That's two strong heartbeats. You're definitely having twins."

The two heartbeats that were lost a week ago were somehow now beating loud and strong. We could see the tiny little specks on the screen pulsing with each beat, quickly supplying life to our two new little babies. Our entire world had completely flipped in a matter of minutes. Our emotions were all over the place, and we could barely communicate with each other without fumbling over ourselves.

Brandon, who had been standing next to me with a tight grip on my hand, sat down to gather himself. The tech continued to measure the babies and check on all the things that come with being pregnant with twins when she suddenly froze.

"Oh my God, there's another one."

"There's another what?"

"There's another baby. You're having triplets. I need to get the doctor."

I've never been at a loss for words; not once in my entire life have I been left speechless. I always have a quick-witted comeback or something funny to say. But I lay there completely stunned. Before I knew it the room had filled with the entire office staff, from the doctors to the receptionist. I was suddenly surrounded by three doctors and a handful of nurses all glued to the screen where they watched the movements of three tiny babies. Some were giggling because it was just so crazy and some were in complete shock. Everyone in the room knew we had walked in there thinking we had lost two little lives. But now, all of us were watching three lives in me thrive.

After what seemed like an hour of measuring and counting again, the doctor asked to speak with us privately in his office. With full hearts we took our seats across from his desk and readied ourselves for a plan of action. We were aware that this was going to be a long and dangerous road. We knew that we would need to take extra precautions and monitor this pregnancy more closely than a normal one. But we weren't prepared for his speech. He explained that the previous week he had seen one small sack and one large, neither with heartbeats. He had assumed that one stopped growing, which would explain why one was bigger than the other. But the lack of heartbeats was because we were too early into the pregnancy.

We then sat in stunned silence as he told us he was going to put me on light bed rest starting now and full bed rest from twenty-five weeks on. His plan was to deliver the babies at thirty-two weeks no matter what and that we would be in for a weekly sonogram.

After detailing what our pregnancy with triplets would look like and all that could go wrong, he suggested that we terminate one of the babies in an effort to give the others a better chance. Two of them were in one sack and categorized as identical twins, and the other was in a separate sack and categorized as their fraternal twin. He gave us the option of reducing it down to either the one that was by itself or the two that were together. He referred to it as selective reduction. In that moment, I knew that we were without a doubt in the wrong place with the wrong doctor. After everything we had gone through in that short week, this man sat across from us and suggested that we end the life of one of these precious babies. I wasn't angry. I was hurt and confused and just wanted out. We thanked him for his time and left, and before we had even made it to the elevator I was on the phone with the doctor I had trusted all my life, the doctor who had delivered me and my daughter. I knew he would make the right decisions for us. We set an appointment with him for the following day.

When we got into the car we took a deep breath and tried to process all that had just happened and what we had ahead of us. We each took a minute to text our families, who had been nervously waiting for us to get out of what they thought would be the worst appointment of our lives. I texted my brother's wife and told her that we were pregnant with triplets. Her response: *"Holy cow, you're having a litter!"*

And technically we were.

When we got home we sat my daughter down to break the news to her. I reminded her of how she prayed that God would put a baby in my tummy. I took her hand and told her that her prayers had been answered and that God had put three babies in my tummy. She took a deep breath, dropped her shoulder, and looked up at me.

"Am I in trouble for praying too hard?"

My little girl, whom I had failed to raise in a Christian home, knew without a doubt that God had not only heard her prayers but also blessed her three times over. In that moment, I knew I wanted what she had. I wanted faith like the five-year-old little girl who confidently sent her prayers to heaven. I wanted the faith of a child.

## A Downhill Spiral

After thirty-five weeks of a fairly uneventful pregnancy, we delivered three healthy baby girls, each weighing over five pounds. And after a short stay in the NICU, we had the whole family home nine days after they came into the world.

Seeing their sweet little faces made my heart ache. This huge and rare life event was something that brought great joy, but I was missing something. The fact that I had given birth to spontaneous multiples was a blessing that was passed down to me through genetics. My dad was a twin; it ran in his family. In some way these three babies were a gift from my dad's side of the family, and I wanted him to share in the joy. I wanted pictures of my dad and his twin brother with arms full of our precious new triplets. I wanted to document the amazingness of my dad and my children being multiples. Deep inside I knew it could never happen, but I ached for just a glimpse of it. My children and my family were surrounded by love and well cared for, but the truth was that I still wanted my dad. I searched for glimpses of him in the eyes of my three newborn babies and hoped that one day I could heal and be brave enough to let him meet them.

We had prepared ourselves the best we could for our family to double in size in just one day. Our families lavished us with gifts and everything we needed for them to come home. We had a freezer full of food, and a pantry stocked with necessities. For the first two weeks we had a revolving door of people coming over to feed a baby or wash clothes. Some even let us take a nap here and there. The two of us created our own routine of nighttime feedings, allowing the other to sleep. We seemed to have it all under control and appeared to be thriving as a family. We were well fed and the babies were well held, but what others didn't know was that our bank account was dwindling and our marriage was falling apart.

After the babies were born, Brandon was let go at his job. What followed was a string of bad job choices and hard knocks. He began to grow bitter from working so hard and never gaining ground, and I was growing bitter from being home alone with three infants most days and several nights. We were both mentally and physically exhausted beyond anything we had ever faced before. The sleepless nights gave way to neglecting each other physically as husband and wife. The financial struggle resulted in fear and stress that gave way to hardened hearts.

Our first few years as a family were spent dog paddling, trying to keep our heads above water, desperate to reach solid ground. We were stuck out in the middle of the ocean during an epic storm, and there was no dry land in sight.

It didn't take long before we lost touch with each other and became simply two people living in the same house. On very rare occasions we would get moments to ourselves, and we could hardly think of anything to talk about. If we talked about the babies, we were sabotaging our free time; if we talked about our marriage, our hearts grew hateful. We had somehow gone from two lovers dancing alone in the dark of the restaurant to two people trying to keep our lives from completely deconstructing.

# EIGHT

# God Turns Sand into a Solid Foundation

A year into our marriage I started to take the kids to the church across the street. I wasn't trying to be a good mom. I just needed the break it gave me from the kids. My cousin had also signed our oldest daughter up for choir, so I was forced to take her to practice.

Every Wednesday night I would stick two of the triplets in a double stroller and balance one on my hip. I would drop their big sister at choir and then I would drop them in childcare. Once there were no longer children hanging on me, I would go to the lobby of the church and just sit. I placed a book in front of me but never read a single word. (The book was simply to deter others from approaching.) I sat with a blank stare and did my best not to cry. I didn't want to make friends there; I just wanted to sit and be silent. I had no intention of getting involved or becoming "one of them." I wasn't like them, and

I knew I never would be. If they tried to create a relationship with me, it would only be a matter of time before they saw how dark I was and what a mess I had made of my life. In my eyes, the people who walked the halls of the church had their lives together. I didn't fit in and so didn't try.

After a year of going every Wednesday night, I started the same routine on Sunday mornings. I would sneak in, as much as anyone can with three babies and a seven-year-old, and after dropping them off I would tiptoe to the back of the worship center and listen to the sermon. Out of respect, I stood when the hymns played but never opened my mouth. I bowed my head as if to pray but my mind was empty. God blessed our marriage with these babies, and we were making a complete mess of it. Why now? Why would I believe after all this that God was going to come in and fix everything? I thought back to those seven days I had lain in bed and made promises to him, and I knew he was looking at me with disappointment. I had broken every promise I had made. Just like every other time in my life, I had failed miserably and didn't want God to see me this way. So I hid in the shadows and took a break from the world for one hour each Sunday morning without a single expectation of getting anything from it.

But God doesn't work that way. He doesn't watch a mother in despair show up in his house every Sunday without doing something about it. I might not have spoken a single word when I was in that building, but God doesn't listen to our mouths. He hears our hearts, and mine was screaming for mercy. My heart was pleading with God even though my head fought it. I was so tired. I had nothing left in me. I hadn't fully accepted the fact that God was real and that he loved me, but every time I showed up to that church a little piece of me was changed.

My life was a mess and I needed help. My husband had no desire to ever attend church with his family, and I didn't want to be married to a man that wouldn't make that sacrifice for me. He was tired too and had given up on me. I gave everything that I had to our children and completely neglected him as a man. I failed him as a wife, and even though I knew I was doing it, I didn't know how to change it. I had made him feel small and insignificant. It wasn't intentional; I loved him. I just didn't know how to survive what we were going through and let him be the man of the house at the same time. Our marriage was spiraling out of control, and I didn't know how to fix it.

## Quicksand

In the spring of 2010, one of our triplets was diagnosed with autism. Even though we had known it in our hearts, seeing it on official documents completely broke us. We had reached a point in our marriage where we no longer knew how to comfort each other. This was another hit that we couldn't seem to recover from. We rallied to make sure we made the right choices for our daughter and gave her the best chances at life, but we could barely look each other in the eyes. How were we going to be the parents she needed when we couldn't even be good people to each other? Something was about to break, and our kids would be the ones to feel the snap.

On Father's Day, June 20, 2010, we loaded the kids in the car and tried to act normal. We attempted a family outing to go see a movie and did our best to be polite to each other. We both knew our marriage was dry and we had nothing to hydrate it, but we played nice for the kids' sake. As we drove past the church I had reluctantly yet faithfully been attending, I turned to him and said, "At least I'm not making you go there today."

At a red light when the car had come to a complete stop, he turned his face to mine and with absolutely no emotions responded, "I hope you know that I will never step foot in that church and I hope you know why."

There was something different in his eyes that day. I knew he had thrown in the towel and was completely at a loss with me. Not even the little ears that were listening from the backseat were enough for him not to put me in my place.

I'm not sure that either one of us spoke another word to each other that day, and our children bore the brunt of it. They went to the movies with a mom and dad who refused to speak to each other aside from ordering the snacks.

We both knew it was coming. On July 13, 2010, at six in the morning we stood face-to-face in our kitchen discussing divorce. Our hearts were bitter and our pride was crushed, but neither of us so much as raised our voice. That was the day I found out infidelity had hit my marriage. Even though I knew we were struggling and had lost our connection with each other, the reality of it stole the air from my lungs and made me want to pass out. All my life I had considered this the number one deal breaker but standing face-to-face, while our children slept in the next room, an entirely different feeling came over me—complete loss. Realizing what we had done to our marriage over the years turned my anger into deep sadness. I knew that the level of forgiveness we needed to save our family was more than either of us possessed.

There was no yelling or fighting. We were both deflated and completely exhausted. I put all the blame on him because it was easier for me, and he took it. He had completely given up. I understood why but my instinct was still to point the finger. We had so much to discuss, but we both just stood there and stared at each other, neither of us able to fully pull the trigger.

In the middle of talking about dismantling the family that I had literally begged God for, I began to sweat. The heat in the house was intense, and both of our shirts were wet with perspiration. In the Texas summer heat, our air conditioner had completely quit on us. We were forced to stop talking about divorce and start working together to figure out what we needed to do to get the kids to day care and get someone in the house to fix the problem. The problem in our marriage was put on the back burner while we faced yet another hit in life.

For three days we were without AC, and the house reached unbearable temperatures. The only room that was cool was the master bedroom due to a small window unit capable of cooling only the one room. We made a makeshift bed on the floor in our room and all piled in for movie night and to sleep together in the only cool place in the house. Brandon and I were forced to pretend like everything was okay. He couldn't bail on us and sleep on the couch; it was simply too hot. I couldn't make him watch TV in the other room; I was mad, not cruel. So, for two nights we were shoved into that room—in the middle of the worst moment in our marriage—and forced to treat each other with respect and kindness for the first time in a long time.

On the third night while I lay in bed waiting for Brandon to come home from work, I heard God speak to me for the first time in my life. From the moment we decided to divorce, I had been pleading with God to fix what was broken. I asked him to give me an out and not make me the bad guy. I questioned why he had put us together in the first place and why he would allow this in our lives. He spoke to me but told me what I didn't want to hear.

That first time I heard God speak to me made me want to plug my ears. Though I had been begging for this moment my entire life, it was about to hit me harder than I expected. I heard him say my name for the first time. He whispered how much he loved me but also told me that I didn't have the right to bail on my husband and my marriage. He gently reminded me of the promises I made those seven days in bed, begging for the lives of my children, and that now was the time to make good on them. He let me know that even in those moments when I didn't believe he was listening and had only cried out in despair, he was there and listening. He had heard me.

He heard me the day I said his name on the way to the lake in the speeding car with my drunk dad behind the wheel. He heard me when I cried out his name in fear of being alone in that big house. He heard me when I begged not to be the invisible girl at the father-daughter dance. He heard me when I pleaded for the lives of the unborn children whose heartbeats couldn't be heard. That night as I asked God to take away the hurt, he let me know that I had been given mercy and forgiveness and that now it was my turn. My job, as the Christian—though conflicted—I had slowly become, was to show my husband what true forgiveness and grace looked like. No matter how much it hurt or how difficult it was, God instructed me to stay and fix what I had broken. My instinct had always been to run, even when I knew I was in the wrong, and never back down or admit my faults. But God was about to teach me how to be a humble and forgiving wife, and I was terrified. He was going to show me what being his daughter was all about.

This wasn't going to be easy. No one would blame either of us if we chose to walk away. But I knew for the very first time that my obedience to God wasn't about me and what I wanted; it was about loving others more than I loved myself. It was about walking through the fire and coming out the other side rather than turning and running to avoid the pain.

When Brandon got home that night, he walked into a cool house. By the grace of God, our AC had been fixed a day earlier than scheduled. He reluctantly made his way to our bedroom and peeked in the door, checking whether I had fallen asleep or was waiting to hammer him some more about our marriage. The kids were finally able to sleep in their own rooms, but that gave us little comfort. Neither of us knew if that meant he would be spending the night on the couch or if we were going to keep up the act for the kids. I saw the door crack open and, with a transformed heart, asked him to come lie next to me. I saw a hint of relief in his eyes, and my heart broke for what must have been going through his mind. I placed my hand on his cheek and, as gently as I could, simply told him that I was his wife and I wasn't going anywhere. Whatever we had been through and whatever we were about to face, I was his wife. For the first time in my life I obeyed God and followed his will instead of my own, and my husband and I spent the rest of the night in tears, apologizing for what we had done to each other and to our family. We stayed up for hours finally talking about what was broken and trying to figure out how to fix it.

Two nights later and after more tears and conversations, Brandon asked if he could attend church the next Sunday with me and the kids. I made sure that his request was about what was on his heart and not what he thought I wanted. I no longer wanted him to do what I wanted him to do. I had willingly, though with difficulty, turned my will over to God and trusted whatever path he was going to put us on, no matter what it looked like. I had finally come to a place in my life where I didn't want to control anyone else or convince them to do what I wanted. I simply wanted God's plan and nothing more.

That Sunday, only a few weeks after he had told me he would never step foot in church, my husband held my hand and walked through the church doors with me. Our girls led him down the hall to their classroom and showed him where they had been learning all about Jesus. I took him to the dark corner of the worship center where I had been hiding out for over a year, and we sat down together and prepared for the service. Until that day, I was still going through the motions at church, standing when I was supposed to stand, sitting when I was supposed to sit, and blankly staring at the preacher while he gave his prepared sermon. But this day something changed. My husband was next to me for the first time, and I didn't feel little or alone. When the preacher stood to speak, I laced my fingers through my husband's and intently listened for the first time. It was as if the preacher had been living in our home for the past few years and knew everything we had gone through. He knew the heavy wounds on our hearts and spoke about forgiveness and grace. He told us about letting go of the past and preparing for the future. His words seemed to be specifically for us and our situation, because that's how the Holy Spirit works. It was designed for us. God had this planned all along, and in that moment I realized that everything we had gone through was for a purpose. We were now going to live through the hurt and understand why we had made it through the fire. I told Brandon that he didn't have to do all the "churchy" stuff while there, but he stood when he was supposed to stand, sat when he was supposed to sit, and bowed his head when we prayed. I don't know what he said to God that day, that's between them, but I do know that God changed something in him too.

When we got in the car after the service was over and started to make our way to lunch, our sweet little girl, who had just a month before been diagnosed with autism, spoke up from the backseat.

"Daddy?"

"Yes, baby?" he said.

"I sing like God."

Her voice and faith in God helped me understand that everything was going to be okay. We would survive and thrive through her diagnosis. Our bank account would somehow replenish. With hard work and massive amounts of grace, our marriage would not only make it through the fire, it would recover from the burns and become new and beautiful again. I didn't know what Brandon's future in the church looked like, but I knew that God was listening to my prayers. I knew for the first time that God knew my name.

Brandon willingly attended church with us again the following Sunday and, just like the week before, he stood when he was supposed to stand and sat when he was supposed to sit. However, something was different. I watched his mouth move with the words of the music, and when he bowed his head to pray, I could hear a faint whisper. I tried to wrap my head around what was happening and wanted to believe that it was genuine, but God transforming hearts had always been an out-of-reach miracle, stuff that didn't happen to people like us. On that day, when the preacher gave the invitation to accept Christ, my husband took my hand and told me he wanted to go down front and speak with a pastor. Just twelve days after we stood face-to-face in our kitchen and decided to divorce, we stood hand-in-hand in front of the entire congregation and I watched as my husband gave his life to Christ. I was grateful and envious at the same time. I had spent many days sitting in those pews, pretending to be all in, but I had never fully committed my life to Christ. I stood and watched this man boldly and confidently accept Jesus as his Savior. With a tight grip on my husband's hand, I confessed my own need for Jesus to live in me. That very same day we signed our name on our membership papers. The church that I had been sneaking in and out of for over a year, the church that my husband vowed to never step foot in, was now our home, and we were both committed to the Lord.

## The Softened Heart of the Believer

On September 12, 2010, Brandon and I were baptized together in front of a thousand strangers who were somehow our new family and the people who would watch us grow in Christ. We didn't know what to expect; we just knew that we wanted to rebuild our family and our lives on a solid foundation. We knew that the center of our marriage would now be God and that we would put him before each other and trust him with the details.

The day of our baptism we took off our old wedding bands and replaced them with new ones. Engraved on each ring are the words "God Be with Us Together and Apart." We placed them on our fingers before we walked to meet each other in the middle of the baptismal pool and to begin our new life together.

Being a believer in Christ doesn't make everything perfect and doesn't take away every struggle. We continue to tread water more than we want, but now we see the shore, and on it stands our Savior. Hard lessons were learned in the early years of our marriage, and what we learned has helped us navigate through the things we face today. No marriage will ever be perfect and ours is certainly nowhere near it, but we have something now that we didn't have before. We have a God of second chances and high doses of mercy. Our marriage may face challenges far greater than we've ever seen—we have no way of knowing—but now we have a peace that can only come from knowing God. His plan is always good, even through the fires, and that is what we remind ourselves on a daily basis. We will walk through many seasons in life. As Brandon's wife, it is my role to support him through those seasons, offer grace, and forgive the way I have been forgiven.

I had no idea how much I was going to truly need this transformation in my heart. I had no idea that God had the power to fill me with the ability to forgive on a level I thought was reserved for people with strength far beyond anything I possessed. God was about to start the healing process that I needed to live my life the way he intended. One of the things he needed to change was how small I felt when standing next to the sins of my dad. In order to heal those wounds, God had to expose them and teach me how to forgive. It would be impossible without the grace of Jesus.

# NINE

# On the Witness Stand

My dad remarried when I turned twenty. I didn't attend the wedding. I wasn't invited and wouldn't have gone even if an invitation had miraculously shown up in my mailbox. Even though I still had a burning desire for his approval, the stone wall I had built up around me allowed very few people in, and even fewer people knew my true feelings.

He started over and left me in the dust. He began to build a new family. My brother was born shortly after his wedding and another brother followed two years later. I was comfortable with that. I refused to have anything to do with his new family, not because I couldn't love my siblings but because being around them meant I had to be around my dad and I couldn't do it. When his wife became pregnant with their third child, I begged God not to let it be a girl. I was afraid of being replaced and completely forgotten, but they had a baby girl in December of 1998. I was twenty-three years old and done with everything that my dad encompassed. He had what he wanted, and I wasn't included.

I made a very conscious effort to make sure his life didn't spill over into mine. I not only cut him off but also avoided him and his new family at any cost. I simply went on with my life as if none of them even existed. He was parenting his children as I was parenting my own. We had weird parallel lives going on that I made sure never intersected.

Then one afternoon in 2006, my phone rang and my step-mom was on the other end. We rarely spoke, and I knew there had to be a serious reason she would dare call me. I hadn't been kind to her and had very little sympathy for her tumultuous marriage to my dad. She had never been able to understand why I refused a relationship with him, and I refused to explain myself to her. But this day her voice quivered and I agreed to listen. I listened to her for over an hour. She explained to me in great detail what had been going on in their lives and what was happening to my siblings. She told me stories that were all too familiar. I had been so bitter about his new family, thinking he had somehow started over and was doing it right this time, but now I learned that he was no better a father to them than he was to me and my older brother.

She finally got to the point of her phone call. She had filed for divorce and had a custody hearing for the three kids. She wanted me to be a witness, to testify against my father at the custody hearing and do whatever I could to make sure he didn't get custody of the kids. I agreed without thinking it through or thinking about what effect it might have on my own emotions. I knew without a doubt that no matter how I felt about him starting a new life, I had to defend my siblings who were at his mercy.

The morning of the hearing, I panicked. I was going to see my dad for the first time in many years and in some twisted way, I wanted to look pretty. Nothing about the day had anything to do with me, but I desperately wanted him to think I was pretty. I would be testifying against him in a few short hours and here I was, standing in the middle of my room with clothes thrown everywhere, trying to decide what I looked best in. I was pathetic.

I had given birth to triplets only months before, and my confidence was still recovering from what my body had gone through. Nothing fit right, I had bags under my eyes, and no amount of coffee could make me look fresh and ready. My emotions were running wild, and I couldn't shake the need to somehow please my dad while crushing him at the same time. I finally settled on a long black skirt, boots, and an oversized sweater that gave me enough room to be comfortable without looking like a complete mess. I gave myself one last check in the mirror, added more concealer under my eyes, and got in my car to drive to the neighboring city where the hearing would take place.

The car ride was twenty minutes, and I fought with myself the entire time. Was I doing the right thing? How could a daughter do this to her dad? Was I going to be an embarrassment to him, or would he be glad to see me no matter why I was there? I couldn't take my mind off the real truth. This wasn't about me or about my dad approving of me.

But everything in me was so desperate. I had only ever had glimpses of my siblings. We had run into each other at random places in our small town and a few times in a restaurant, but we had never spent any real time together. I figured they either wouldn't be at the hearing or wouldn't know who I was. The thought of communicating with them wasn't even in my head; I was too wrapped up in what my dad was going to do.

I agreed to meet my stepmom in the parking lot across from the courthouse so we could go over what was going to happen before we went inside. As I pulled into the empty spot next to her, I saw three little faces pressed against the window, waiting for me. I slowly got out of my car and all at once, all three of my sweet younger siblings ran toward me. They didn't carry the baggage and fears that I did. They didn't harbor resentment toward me the way that I did them. They were excited to see me. Six little arms wrapped themselves around my waist and squeezed as hard as they could. It was as if they knew nothing but absolute love for me, and I knew in that moment why I was there.

I was doing the right thing.

It wasn't about the outfit I had chosen or the six cups of coffee I had consumed in an effort to make me look awake. It wasn't about my relationship with my dad or lack thereof. It wasn't about what he had done to me and the father he had failed to be. It was about saving these three innocent children from even a drop of what he had put me through. It was about not allowing my dad to do to my little sister what he had done to me. It was about them, and I fully accepted that.

I gave them hugs and told them I loved them, and then their uncle came to pick them up. We didn't want them to be in court while the hearing took place. An attorney on their behalf would be present to make sure they were taken care of in the best way possible. After we watched them drive away we headed into court. My heart was beating so hard that it hurt my chest. I wasn't sure what to expect, and I was terrified to see my dad. I was afraid he would convince me—of what I wasn't sure—but I knew I didn't trust myself around him. I was a wreck.

We were led into a side room to go over things with my stepmom's lawyer before court started. The room was larger than it looked from the outside and boasted a huge wooden table with ten chairs surrounding it. There was a semi-fancy water carafe on the table with a few tall glasses. A massive picture of a landscape hung on the wall opposite the door, making it the first thing you saw when you walked in. The room seemed to be decorated to make people comfortable, but it still felt official.

I stood awkwardly waiting for someone to signal where I should sit. For the first time in my life I found comfort in my stepmom. She was the only familiar face in the room, and I gravitated in her direction. I didn't necessarily want her to put her arm around me or anything like that, but I needed her close.

We sat in that room for what seemed like hours, going over details of what was going to happen once we made our way into the courtroom. One of the lawyers asked me to tell him a little about my life growing up with my dad and that was all I needed to spill it all to them. With each new story I told, their jaws dropped a little lower. From a lawyer's perspective, I'm sure it was pure gold. They were, after all, headed into a custody case and wanted ammo against the defendant. From my perspective, it was a tragedy. Even though I was a grown adult, it still stung each time I talked about it. As bravely as I could I told them as much as I could remember, and they loaded their notepads with enough information to win the fight. I knew it was what I had to do to help my siblings; I had to remove my own personal hurt and ignore the smiles on the men who were elated to have this new information.

After what seemed like the bulk of the day, we headed into the courtroom to begin the hearing. They had informed me that my dad would be representing himself. I laughed at his arrogance. What kind of person represents himself in his own custody case? It was comical and sad at the same time.

Everyone made their way to the front and sat in their designated spots before the judge. I sat as far back as I could, trying to hide from my dad. He caught a glimpse of me and simply went on about his business, assuming I was there to support my stepmom.

When the trial began, his confidence blew me away. How does he pull it off? How does he stand in front of all these people and pretend to know what he's doing? He's brilliant. He's always been the smartest person I know. Had he put in real work, I can't imagine the levels he could have reached. He was smart, but he was also defiant and thought he was better than everyone. That was his handicap. He thought his good looks, smooth tongue, and quick wit were enough. He had been in so many legal battles that he had become well acquainted with the law and oddly knew more than some lawyers. He was the smartest idiot I'd ever known.

He walked confidently around the courtroom stating his case and cross-examining the people who were there in defense of the kids. He had a stack of legal papers and referred to them often. He was good, and for a split second I wanted to clap for him. For a split second, I was proud of how smart he was and how well he was doing. For being a self-educated man, he sure could fake being a lawyer. He had such poise and confidence. Even I was convinced.

As soon as his grandstanding was done, the lawyer for my stepmom took his place in front of the courtroom. He began by calling my stepmom to the stand. I watched my dad give a small chuckle. She was no match for him. He could twist her until she bent in the direction he wanted her to go. Her time on the witness stand was short and for good reason. Her lawyer didn't want her caught in my dad's crosshairs. He got her up there and down again as quickly as he could. I could tell my dad had a sense that he was winning, and I saw his chest puff up a little.

Just as my dad was getting comfortable in his seat, the lawyer called my name. "I would like to call Candice Curry to the stand."

I took an extra second to watch my dad's reaction. He let out every trace of air he had just used to puff up his chest, put his face in his hands, and shook his head. He had thought I was there simply to support my stepmom. Never in a million years did he think I would be brave enough to take the stand. I stood and adjusted my skirt. I had to silently encourage my feet to make the walk that led to the witness stand. I wondered what everyone was thinking and whether those who didn't know me had figured out that the defendant's daughter had just taken the stand against him in his custody hearing. I had to remind myself that this was not about me and that I was there to protect my siblings. I wanted it to be about me. I wanted to get up there and throw things in my dad's face. I wanted to cry for myself and everything I had lost. Instead, I tilted my head back slightly before I opened the half gate that led to the stand. The last thing I wanted was for my dad to see my fear and pain. I sat down and turned my body slightly toward the judge so that more of my back would face my dad. It gave me security.

The first lawyer approached and began asking me questions.

"Mrs. Curry, is Richard Snell your father?"

"Inside this courtroom, and for the purpose of this hearing, he is. Outside of this courtroom, he is not."

From the corner of my eye I watched my father bow his head.

The lawyer was full of confidence and armed with the information I had given him only an hour before. He used every story he had heard in that big room. Almost all of my life was being laid out in that courtroom and, even though I knew it had to be done, I was dying inside. I couldn't look at my dad, who was sitting closer to me than the lawyers I had befriended.

When the lawyer was done he thanked the judge and took his seat. I knew what was coming next. The judge turned to my dad and let him know it was his turn to proceed. I swallowed the lump in my throat so loudly it made my stepmom look up and smile at me to try to ease my fears.

He fumbled through a few papers as if he had prepared something for this moment. The truth is he'd had no idea I would be there, and he began to panic. He had chosen to defend himself in his own custody hearing and here he was face-to-face with his adult daughter whom, he knew, he had mentally and emotionally beaten down for years. He knew I had more on him than he cared to let loose that day, and he needed a minute to think about how he was going to pull off controlling my answers. As he flipped page after page, buying himself some time, my heart shattered into a million pieces. In my head I was almost cheering him on, wanting him to find something to use against me. I knew my thoughts were crazy, but I didn't want to see him fail or panic as he was in front of me now. It was killing me. I was devastated for him.

*Come on, Dad. Find something. Find anything.* I was betting against myself, but it was emotionally easier than betting against him.

We hadn't spoken in years. I had completely removed him from my life for the sake of my family. I knew I could go the rest of my life setting myself up for disappointment, but I couldn't set my family up for it. And now here we were, finally able to speak to each other but in one of the worst scenarios possible. He would have to cross-examine me in his custody hearing. He would have to face the fact that not only had he lost me, he was also about to lose his other daughter. But this wasn't about either of us. It wasn't about me and it wasn't about him. This was about three children who needed a hero. They needed someone to stand up for them and not allow the abuse to continue. I chose to sacrifice any emotions I had so that I could be that someone. Everything in me needed to make sure my little sister didn't meet the same fate I had.

He slowly approached me.

"Mrs. Curry, isn't it true that you wanted to live with me when your mother and I got a divorce?"

And with that he opened the floodgates. For once in my life I didn't back down or hold anything back.

He questioned me in such a way as to maneuver me to answer the way he wanted. I refused. He's the one who taught me how to word things in a way that would put me in the right every time. He taught me the art of manipulation, and now it was helping me beat him at his own game. Question after question I shot down his motive, and each time he walked over to his desk and fumbled through his stack of papers. It was the saddest and most satisfying thing I've ever done in my life. The daughter in me wanted him to win, wanted him to be this amazing father who was fighting for the right to see his children. I wanted him to come off as true and genuine, so much so that the judge complimented him on his parenting skills. However, the grown woman, mom, and big sister in me needed to put him in his place. I needed to show him that he was no longer going to control me and that he was not going to do to my siblings what he had done to me. I needed to show him that it was over—for good this time.

It took everything I had to do the right thing as I sat in that witness chair. I had to physically make myself look him in the eyes and not show weakness or sympathy. It felt like I was watching a movie because this just couldn't be happening. Who cross-examines his own child in his custody case? It takes a true narcissist to think you can manipulate that many people, including the one who knew most of your secrets, into thinking you are something different from what you really are.

That was my dad's specialty. He could make you think whatever he wanted you to think. When you knew something was wrong, he made you think it was right. It's the talent of a sociopath. He could be so convincing that in order not to be lured by his lies, you had to completely remove yourself from his aim. My siblings were too little to move out of his line of fire, but I wasn't. I was big enough to pick them up and move them to safety. That's why I sat in that witness box that day.

I watched my dad fumble through the papers a little longer after answering each question, and I knew he was at a complete loss. He would have thrown anything he could my way. He wasn't concerned about sparing my dignity or guarding my heart, and it didn't matter that it was his own child sitting in front of him. He was cutthroat. Nothing ever stood in the way of my dad getting what he wanted. The consequences of his actions never mattered. He tried to get me to answer each question in his favor, but I responded in my siblings' favor, refusing to play his games. One side of me got great satisfaction watching him become exhausted; the other side begged him to give up. But I wasn't going to be the one to throw in the towel. I was in it for the long haul and prepared to answer his questions for as long as he was prepared to ask them.

Finally, he walked back to his designated table, shut his folder, and told the judge he was done. Defeat was written all over his face, so much so that the entire courtroom knew he had just destroyed himself in his own custody case. I didn't do it; he did it to himself. My words definitely hurt his case, but he's the one who had spent my entire life being a father who had no business parenting a child. He destroyed his right to a relationship with his children; I just brought the truth to light. I had to remind myself of this several times throughout the day. The guilt I felt was overwhelming, causing me to become nauseated. Seeing him give up and tell the judge he was done both angered and relieved me at the same time. How could he be done? Wasn't he willing to fight to the end for his kids? He should have continued standing at my side rebutting everything I said until I caved and ran from the room in tears. That's how hard I wanted him to fight for my siblings. I wanted them to know he had done everything he could.

But the end of the questioning was a relief as well. It meant I was free to go. I didn't have to sit there for another minute in a state of panic. My relief, however, was his defeat, and that didn't feel as good as I had expected it to. The thirteen-year-old me wanted to jump from the stand, run to him, and fall to his feet, apologizing for what I had just done. The thirteen-year-old me wanted to sob in my hands until the courtroom filled with my tears, forcing everyone else to hold their breath the way I had held mine. But I wasn't thirteen, and I had said good-bye to the little girl who was desperate for her dad many years before. I needed to leave her behind and move forward. I had already mourned the loss of what he failed to give me as a father. It was time to accept that I was never going to get it. The thirty-one-year-old me had to be a big girl.

My siblings' lawyers and my stepmom wore huge smiles. I was completely conflicted. I felt like walking over and spitting in their faces. They had the right to wear those smiles; they had done exactly what they were there to do. But it was at my dad's expense and that infuriated me.

I had been cheering them on, hoping they would win big, but their win cut me in a way I didn't expect. My dad had no one on his team. Not a single person was there in his defense, and not a single person sat next to him during the hearing. He brought this on himself, yet it was still a gut-wrenching sight. How does someone go an entire lifetime and end up with nobody and nothing to show for it? How does a man with seven siblings, five children, and six grandchildren not have anyone to support him? He stood in a sad and lonely place. Had I not been a wife and mother I might have caved. If I had only myself to look out for, I probably would have gone to him and formed a covenant between the two of us. That's how weak I was as my dad's daughter. But as a wife to Brandon and mother to Stiles, Myleigh, Justin, and Bella, I was a deeply rooted tree, bending but never breaking.

I took a deep breath and let it out as slowly as possible so no one in the room would hear. Just as I was about to get up, the judge turned toward me and said, "Mrs. Curry, what do you think Mr. Snell's visitation with his kids should be?"

Suddenly, without notice, the ball was back in my court. It was not something I was prepared for. I didn't want to answer in front of my dad, and I didn't have time to compose my words in a way that wouldn't cut him to the bone. I wished I hadn't sounded so confident earlier. Maybe the judge would have spared me the question.

My dad looked down; he knew what was coming. But every other head in the courtroom perked up, eager to hear my response. The shake in my voice would have registered on the Richter scale.

I turned to the judge and told him that my dad shouldn't get any visitation with his children, but if he did, it should be minimal and supervised.

I kept my face toward the judge, hoping my words would meet only his ears and no one else's. I reiterated that my dad had a way with words and was a master promise maker and breaker. If alone with the kids, he would lie to them, make grand promises that he would never keep, and cheat them out of the good and honest dad that they deserved. He would buy their time and attention with things he stole from others. The kids needed a middleman. They needed someone to buffer the visits and protect them from my dad's games.

I had nothing left to wrap up my thoughts on his visitation; I merely stared at the judge with pleading eyes, silently begging him to let me leave. My normal reaction in a situation like this would be to cry. Tears would sneak up on me and, no matter how hard I tried to contain them, would let loose like rushing water from the floodgates. But my eyes were dry. Not a single tear formed, not even ones that I had to fight to keep in. I felt empty.

"Mrs. Curry, you're free to go."

I froze. Numb. Lost.

What just happened?

In just thirty minutes I had destroyed my dad. It took the exact same amount of time to protect my siblings and save them from what my older brother and I had suffered. There was victory in that courtroom, but not for me and not for my dad. The lawyers knew they had won the minute I took the stand. There wasn't a single person in that room who had any doubt what my dad's visitation rights would be, and there was no doubt about who had provided the key factor in the decision. I was a twisted hero for the lawyers and a nightmare for my dad. Neither felt good.

*"Mrs. Curry, you're free to go."*

I was free to go.

I was free.

I snapped back to reality. I needed to move. Get up. Take my freedom and leave. Without making eye contact with anyone in the room, I got up from the witness stand and quickly made my way out of the courtroom.

I had spent my time in the witness stand listening to my dad try to manipulate me into lying for him like he had done my entire life. He listened while I told a room full of people that he didn't deserve to be a dad. Everything between us ended that day. That was the last time I ever spoke to my dad.

# TEN

# In the Blink of an Eye

Five years passed after testifying against my dad, and neither of us made any effort to fix our relationship. I caught a brief glimpse of him at my aunt's funeral three years after the hearing, but I refused to make eye contact or even offer him condolences for the loss of his sister. I tried to bury everything from that day in court and move forward with my family. I simply went about my life as if he didn't exist.

Rain lightly tapped on our roof and I could hear the gentle swishing of the nebulizer that was secured to my daughter's face. These are the days that I wish I were a stay-at-home mom, so I could nurse my daughter back to health. Instead, I would drive around town all day selling food to restaurants. I would have liked to call in, but I was responsible for someone else's territory and had no choice but to head to work. Thankfully, my husband was able to stay home with her. Even though that gave me some level of comfort, it didn't take away the pain of having to leave my little girl while she was so sick.

I headed out the door with my computer bag and a thousand pounds of guilt. The day consisted of halfhearted work and numerous phone calls home. I rushed about, doing just enough to get by and not get in trouble with my boss. I finally made my way back home in time to start dinner and give my daughter another breathing treatment.

In the back of my mind I debated whether to take her to the emergency room or fight her asthma through the night in the comfort of our home. This wasn't the first time we'd been faced with this decision. Our youngest triplet has battled weak lungs since birth, and we've spent more nights sharing a hospital bed with her than we care to count. The decision to go or stay and do treatments every two to four hours is always a struggle. Tonight I leaned toward going and started packing an overnight bag just in case.

As I got her comfortable on the couch and headed to my room to pack, the phone rang. The screen showed it was my brother. It was odd because he rarely called in the middle of dinnertime, but I figured he was calling to check on his niece.

"Hello?"

"What are you doing?"

"Taking Bella to the hospital."

"Okay, hold on, I need to tell you something."

And then everything froze as I listened to my brother's strong yet gentle voice come through the phone.

"Dad just killed himself."

From the other room Brandon heard me repeatedly crying, "No, no. Oh my God!" As my knees buckled and I went to the floor, he came into our room and sat down next to me. I could faintly hear my brother on the other end of the line telling me it was okay, but we both knew it wasn't.

Brandon sat there for several minutes and listened helplessly as I repeated the same words over and over. "No, no. Oh my God!" The hardwood floor beneath me offered little comfort, nor did the voices around me saying it was going to be all right. My face was pressed against the cold floor. Suddenly everything in my life looked different.

After what seemed like forever, my brother and I agreed on the phone calls each of us would make and said that we loved each other. I hung up and glanced at the dial pad on my phone. Reluctantly I called my mom's cell phone and prayed she wouldn't answer. In that moment, I needed someone else to break the news. I didn't want to be responsible and gentle. I wanted to kick and scream and have someone else handle the hard things. I wanted to hide under my covers and pretend life wasn't happening this way. In an instant I hated everyone.

My mom was in the middle of dinner at a nice restaurant when I blurted out that my dad had just killed himself. What does a mom do with news like that? How on earth do you comfort your child, even if she's an adult, through the suicide of her father? With very little reaction, she told me she was on her way. As she handed the phone to my stepdad, I could hear her telling him what happened. I hung up the phone and sat still.

Brandon was scrambling around trying to get the kids away from our bedroom in an effort to spare them the sound of their mom's cries. He tried to keep normalcy in the house until it was time for them to go to bed. He juggled being a gentle father to our daughters and a strong husband to his wife, who sat in her room with a completely shattered heart. I stayed locked in our bedroom, shaking and crying with my hand over my mouth, praying that might prevent the words from coming out again. I tried to focus on my breathing. It was heavy and labored and I needed to slow it down. I became completely consumed with guilt and grief. I replayed all the hateful words I had ever spoken to him. I saw myself sitting in that courtroom, stealing his time away from his children. I could see myself screaming at him and completely ignoring him. I started to convince myself that this was somehow my fault.

I made calls to work and my close friends and then called my little sister. She was eerily calm and quiet. I wondered if she truly knew what had happened or if her stepdad had softened the blow for her. A twelve-year-old girl sat alone in her bedroom at her mom's house, miles from my reach. How could he do this to her? She shouldn't have to face this. She shouldn't have to hear grownups explain that her dad was gone and, even worse, that he was gone by his own hand. My instinct was to go rescue her, but I wasn't in a position to help anyone else. I was a mess and could hardly keep myself together. I wouldn't have been able to be strong for her.

Slowly my house began to fill with people. I couldn't decide if I needed them there or wanted them all to just go home. I was mad at everyone, even though the person who was truly at fault was gone. I wanted someone to blame, someone to curse and hate. My friends and family came to love on me, but I couldn't pretend to care. One of my friends pulled me into the bathroom, sat down in front of me, and let me just cry and shake my head in grief. Very softly she asked if I had called my dad and told him that I forgave him, something we had talked about me doing only a month before. I continued to shake my head no and felt guilty for not forgiving him. I offered few words on how I was feeling, but words weren't needed. I remained still, staring forward with tears streaming down my face and shaking my head.

Maybe if he had been a good dad, then the people gathered around me would have known what to say. Maybe if he had died a different way, they'd have known how to act. Maybe if they'd liked him, they'd have had the right words. But this was a man that very few people had truly cared about. This was a man that people had intentionally removed from their lives in an effort to protect themselves. I had done exactly the same thing. I wasn't a fool. I knew how everyone in the room felt, and I knew they were truly at a loss for words for very good reason. But I needed to pretend for one second that he was a great loss to everyone.

I went to kiss my daughters goodnight and saw my little girl with the nebulizer mask on her face. How had I forgotten how sick she was? What kind of a mother was I? In my selfish despair, I simply kissed her head and turned to leave. I was a selfish little girl again who didn't want to give any of herself to anyone else, not even the innocent little girl who was struggling to catch a breath. My chest hurt as deeply as hers did, and I struggled to catch my own breath. I didn't bother to hide my tears or wipe them from my face; I let them form a trail behind me as I left her room.

Eventually everyone made their way home and my house stood quiet. I wondered how they could dare leave me like this and gave thanks for them leaving, all at the same time. Brandon was emotionally and physically exhausted from keeping the kids on their normal routine and getting them to bed on time when things were anything but normal. Within minutes of us getting into bed I heard his breathing slow down and become rhythmic. I knew he had fallen asleep. I lay quietly with my eyes wide open for the rest of the night.

Details about how my dad died and how he was found began to emerge early the next morning. My brother picked me up and together we headed to the funeral home to meet our aunt and uncle. My dad's twin brother took the lead for us, as he had done many times throughout our lives. From the time we were small children, he acted as a disciplinarian when we needed it and loved on us the way our dad should have. He tried to help us through life's big decisions and gave as much parental guidance as possible. As my dad's twin, he was the closest person to him, and we viewed him as an extension of our dad. We clung to the hope that somewhere deep inside of our dad he was, on some level, like his brother. Our uncle did his best to stand in the gap our father left wide open in our lives, but he also had a family and kids of his own. We simply couldn't take top priority and we understood.

My brother pulled his truck into the empty spot next to our uncle. We got out without saying a word and got into the backseat of his car, waiting for the funeral home to open. My uncle turned his body toward to us but never made eye contact. I don't know if it was for his own sake, sparing himself from looking into my swollen eyes, or for my sake, sparing me from seeing the face of my father reflected in his. In his most fatherly voice, he asked us if we wanted to know what had happened that night in our dad's hotel room. Simultaneously, I said yes and my brother said no.

My yes must have been louder than my brother's no because my uncle began to detail the last actions of our dad. He gave us the short version, and it sufficed for the moment. I knew I would need more, and if it didn't come from him, I would seek it elsewhere until every corner of my mind was satisfied.

My dad had tied one end of his makeshift noose to the towel bar in a hotel room and the other end around his neck. He then sat down and let it slowly strangle him until he let out his last breath. There wasn't a single sign of struggle. He never once grabbed at his neck in a last ditch effort to save himself. The thought of his five children wasn't enough to make him hook his fingers around his noose and attempt to pull it loose.

He sat there for three days until the maid came to clean his room and discovered what he had done.

My brother, uncle, aunt, and I sat in a tiny room inside the funeral home and made small talk, some about my dad and some about life in general. They did their best to be lighthearted, even sneaking in a joke or two, but my face never changed and the tears never stopped escaping from my eyes, no matter how hard I tried to stop them. Nothing was going to ease the pain I was feeling. It was a toxic mix of grief, guilt, and anger. I was so angry with everyone, especially the people in front of me. They were an easy target and I had a loaded bow, shooting arrows at everyone in my path.

We collectively made the choice of cremation and my uncle wrote a check so that neither my brother nor I would feel the financial burden. He tried to take away the burn of our dad sticking it to us one last time.

As delicately as my aunt could, she asked if we were going to cremate him and be done. I know she meant no harm in it and was only seeking information about our plans, but the question broke me. It reminded me of who and what my dad had truly been, and I wasn't ready to deal with all that. I wasn't ready to set aside the hurt of his suicide and face the realities of his life. I knew that no one liked my dad, many people even hated him, but I hadn't considered that people would choose to quietly say good-bye and then move on, barely even blinking at what had just happened to his children and the gravity it had added to our lives. I knew I couldn't do that. No matter how the world felt about my dad, I had to honor him on some level. It sounded crazy in my own head, so I can only imagine how it sounded when I said it out loud.

This wasn't a mere moment for us. This was a life event that would change who we were forever. It had derailed us, changing the course of what we thought our future lives might look like. Aside from my brother and me, my dad had left three children who had not yet reached adulthood. I needed them to know that it was okay to love our dad and remember him with smiles, that someone loved him enough to hold a funeral in his honor out of respect. I needed them to understand that we can love people from afar and can forgive in all circumstances. I needed them to see people walk into a church and remind them that they are loved. Then again, maybe I did it just for me, because I wanted to pretend that my dad had loved me and I owed it to him.

I saw the shocked look on my brother's face when I said I was going to have a funeral, but his words did not match his expression. I knew it was because he loved me more than he loved himself. He lovingly put his arm on my back and told me that he would do whatever I wanted. He would support me in my decision, like he had done my entire life.

We made arrangements for his cremation and funeral service, and then went to the police station to collect the items our dad had left behind. After a few hours of filling out paperwork and waiting, we walked out with a trash bag full of my dad's belongings. My heart was racing to tear it open and inspect every single item. If it had been up to my brother, we wouldn't have recovered the bag from the evidence room. He wanted nothing to do with anything our dad had left behind.

## Room 101

The moment my brother dropped me off at home, I almost ran to my room and emptied the contents of the bag onto my bed. His clothes, glasses, wallet, and a cane all sat on my bed. On top of the pile a small ziplock plastic bag caught my eye. When I picked it up I didn't expect to get the information I was so desperate for. Written on the bag that contained the $16.34 the detectives pulled from my dad's pocket was the hotel name and room number where they had found him. I had a piece of information in my hand that would slowly start to haunt me.

Room 101.

He took his life in room 101 of a Days Inn that I just happened to pass several times each day when I worked. I knew this hotel and the exit from the highway that led right to it. My desire to go there began to overwhelm me. I couldn't focus on anything except that room. I wasn't new to the feeling of wanting something that I knew was unhealthy for me. The craving I felt for this room was stronger than anything else I had ever felt. I wanted to know the color of the carpet and the layout of the room; the pattern of the bedspread haunted my dreams. I knew deep inside that nothing good would come of me experiencing room 101 for myself. But the need was like a lion to a lamb, and I didn't stand a chance.

Only days after discovering where my dad took his life, I found myself on autopilot in that direction. I was going several miles per hour slower than the rest of the traffic so as not to miss my turn. I didn't notice my breathing speed up as I slowly made the right turn into the Days Inn parking lot. Room 101 was the first to welcome me. Its entrance faced the highway, and as I turned in I almost ran into it.

There it was. I was only a turn of a door handle away from being in the very place my dad took his last breath. Desperation filled me. I parked my car and sat, staring at the door, unable to take my eyes off it. I stared at the door handle to room 101 for almost an hour, wishing I could turn it. I fantasized about booking the room but wondered if my request for that specific room would set off some internal alarm and they'd be on to me.

My dad left so much behind in that room, things invisible to the eyes. He left the shattered hearts of five children. He left questions that would never be answered. Room 101 was where all my worth sat, waiting for someone to rescue it and return it to me.

How was I not enough? If not me, how were my siblings not enough? When he tied that noose around his neck, did pictures of his kids flash through his mind? Did he cry? Did he whisper out loud how sorry he was for what he was about to do to us? How did the visual of my sister's little chubby cheeks not stop him from tying the other end of the rope to the towel bar? He was a grandpa. How did the desperation of wanting to be a part of their lives not make him a better person? How did their precious names not weigh heavily on his heart in that very moment and force him to stand up?

Just stand up.

Why didn't you just stand up?!

Room 101 turned me into a thirteen-year-old girl again, desperate for her dad, desperate for his approval. Desperate.

How?

Why?

*I hate you, room 101.*

I put the car in gear and slowly made my way out of the parking lot, knowing I'd be back. I was a moth and room 101 was my flame.

As I was pulling away I noticed that room 101 was the only room at the hotel that didn't have blinds over the window above the door. It was a half-moon-shaped window and for some reason it was naked. Like a pot of water on a hot stove I slowly began to boil. My feelings were so mixed up and confused. The fact that the place where my dad took his last breath was exposed through a window was too much for me to handle. I needed the window to be covered. I needed the secrets to be hidden.

*Please, God, make them cover the window.*

That simple oversight by the hotel management was added to the list of things I obsessed over after my dad's suicide.

---

Three days after I drove away from the hotel where my dad took his own life, I stood in front of a packed church and delivered his eulogy. The church wasn't packed for him. The church was packed for me, my three brothers, and my little sister who hadn't yet reached her teenage years. Unlike the time I spoke to a packed court about how terrible my dad was at being a dad, this time I had to find a way to speak about the good in him. My knees were shaking uncontrollably, and I made every effort not to make eye contact with my siblings. The last place I wanted to be was standing at the pulpit of my church, where I had been saved only a year before, trying to find the right balance of words not to glorify the man, who had lived unrighteously, but to honor his children. I took a deep breath and let it out.

My dad wore Levi jeans. He wore them with white tennis shoes almost every day. You could probably ask any one of my childhood friends, and they would know what jeans he wore; it was kind of a joke with us. We called them Richard jeans, after my dad. When I was a little girl, I would put my hand in his back pocket so that I wouldn't lose him when we were in public. I never had to look up; I just knew he was there. I grew out of it, or maybe his jeans got too tight for my hand. Either way, my hand didn't fit in his pocket anymore and I lost him. I lost him to a world that I couldn't understand and probably never will. Most of us lost him in our lives at some point.

My dad had a good side and when my dad was good, he was great. My friends always wanted to stay at our house because he was so much fun. He would barge into our rooms at the crack of dawn on a morning after a slumber party with friends and sing a ridiculous song as loud as he could, "Wake up, get out of bed, pull the covers across your head!" He later did the same thing to my younger siblings, except he spared them that stupid song. Then he would make a huge pan of sausage and eggs, something my little sister said he did for her and my little brothers too, so it was clearly something he enjoyed doing for all of his kids. He spent weeks learning the big mac rap on YouTube with my little brothers, and he and Josh became quite good at being rappers. He was Jordan's hunting partner, and of course they always took the fanciest car into the woods to bring the animals back. I once watched them strap a buck to the top of my mom's yellow Cadillac and drive it home.

His brothers and sisters at one time had a fun, adventurous, and extremely wild brother that gave them some amazing memories. I'm sure he has friends that could sit and tell stories about their adventures that would make you question their sanity. My dad had a very loving side to him; he just didn't know how to express it or sometimes did it in the wrong way.

The most amazing thing about God is his amazing grace. God gives us an unconditional love and forgiveness, but I am most thankful that he gave us the ability to forgive not only others but ourselves as well. The last week we have had to face feelings that are more up and down than a roller coaster. The anger, guilt, grief, and overwhelming pity and sadness have gone back and forth without any control. I know that for me, my brothers, and sister this is a time to finally heal, forgive, and move forward, none of which would be possible without God's amazing grace.

When my dad passed away he left nothing behind. My brothers and sister have nothing of his to hold, nothing to pass down to their children, nothing to cherish. I felt desperate to have the clothes that were left in his closet. I was allowed to go to his house and collect his clothes. I'm not sure why this meant so much to me. I asked my friends and family over and over if they thought I was crazy for being so desperate for his clothes. I felt like I was grasping aimlessly for anything that attached me to my dad. When I got to his room it was left just the way that he left it. His last change of clothes were thrown on his bed: a T-shirt, a flannel shirt, and a pair of those Levi jeans.

For one last time, I got to put my hand in the back pocket of my dad's Levi's. I didn't have to look up; I knew he was there.

The last communication anyone had with my dad was an email that he sent to his girlfriend. It was in all capital letters and it read, "TELL MY KIDS THAT I LOVE THEM."

Victoria, Dad loves you.

Joshua, Dad loves you.

Ricardo, Dad loves you.

Jordan, Dad loves you.

# ELEVEN

# The Day the Bricks Came Crashing Down

"Mrs. Curry, we need you to come in first thing tomorrow. Are you able to do that?"

"Come in where? Am I in trouble?" I asked.

My GPS led me to the building by the quickest route possible. I wished there was a setting that would have made it take me the extra-long way. Maybe I should have driven around aimlessly and then called to say I couldn't make it because I was lost. Technically that was true, I was lost, or rather, I was at a loss. The idea that I had been called in to FBI headquarters seemed like something out of a movie.

I parked far enough away to give myself time to think while I made the hike across the parking lot to the front entrance. The cold wind hit me as I opened the car door, and it stole my breath like a thief on a jewelry heist.

*Don't give it back, I thought, sell it to the highest bidder.*

151

Maybe not being able to breathe would make this all go away. But as I felt my chest rise and sink, I knew walking into the building was inevitable. I had no other choice.

I held my head high with what I thought was confidence and walked steadily to the front gate. Even though my mind was telling me that I gave the impression of knowing what I was doing, I knew darn well my steps were more like those of a marionette. It was freezing cold, and I had never been more terrified in my life. My legs forced themselves one in front of the other, awkwardly bending at the knee and swinging each foot forward. My brain fought to turn around, but my legs kept moving as if they were completely unattached to my body. As my mind and body fought against each other, my heart was caught in the middle. After thirty-six years, he still managed to somehow make me his puppet. I still somehow craved his approval.

When I approached the security door, a man's voice came through the small box mounted on the wall. He asked me to send my purse through the bulletproof window that slid open as he spoke. I was instructed to remove my belt and anything that I might have in my pockets. Embarrassed at the contents of my pockets, I slowly set down a stick of gum, a used tissue, and a tube of Chapstick. I wanted the security guard to look up at me and give me a knowing chuckle to ease my fear. I watched him go through my purse, twice, and then I walked through the metal detectors and prayed that the dreaded buzzing didn't go off as I passed through. There was a freedom that came from the silence of the metal detectors. Any attempt thus far to hold me back had failed, and I was slowly going from victim to victory.

I made it to the heavy metal door and pushed the button to be buzzed in. No doubt I had been filmed the entire way from my car to the door. Now that I think about it, I'd probably been followed from my house to the parking lot. Surely they had been watching me, maybe not for weeks or months but definitely from the moment I acknowledged I was his daughter. They had to have tagged me when I mentioned the laptop. I started to convince myself they had microchipped me in the middle of the night while I slept. It's possible that I've watched too many episodes of *Cops* and *Dateline*. The truth was that they just wanted to talk to me. I refused to let my guard down, though, and waste all the years I had spent building up my brick walls, laying each brick one by one, day after day, in an effort to hide behind them. I wasn't going to be had this late in the game. They weren't going to get me. I was ready.

The buzzer sounded and I heard the bolt to the door unlock. I'd only heard those sounds on TV in shows about prisons. The guard always calls out to someone the eye can't see, the buzzing sound comes through, and the guard is able to swing the bars open.

I walked through the door. The room I immediately passed into was a huge circle with nothing on the paneled walls. Nothing about it was inviting. Nothing about it was comfortable. There definitely wasn't a welcome sign. There were three unlabeled doors that blended in with the walls and a front desk. Behind the bulletproof glass at the front desk sat an older woman who seemed to peer at me over her reading glasses. I didn't expect a friendly hello or a hug, but a smile wouldn't have killed her.

I signed in with a shaky hand, my signature almost unrecognizable, showed my ID, and then made the horrible mistake of asking where I could find the restroom. Evidently one of the three mystery doors did not lead to a bathroom. She used the intercom to call someone to the lobby to escort me. A man in a business suit opened one of the doors and guided me down the hall to the ladies' room. He stood outside the entire time I was in there. I felt like I was in the middle of a drug test and felt the pressure of someone watching. He wasn't actually watching me, but I knew he could hear everything I was doing from the other side of the door. I finished and stepped out into the hall where he was patiently waiting. I was hesitant to look him in the eye; it seemed weird that he had just listened to my every move inside the women's restroom. He didn't show any signs of caring and dutifully walked me back to the lobby. I sat down, still creeped out by how the doors blended with the walls and that there wasn't a single sign anywhere to indicate which door led to what.

I wished I could figure out what the scent of the room was and where it was coming from. I love when you can associate a memory with a smell. When I smell vinegar it reminds me of my grandmother's German potato salad. When I smell dryer sheets it takes me back to my best friend's house. I can picture her mom cooking dinner with the clothes washing in the next room. The smell of a popular cologne from 1992 takes me back to my first date. But I couldn't pinpoint the smell in the awkward lobby. Was it old books or fancy leather shoes? Did it smell more like my grandma's house or an uptight store in the open air mall? I'd have to settle on a library and move on, or my mind would catch fire due to sensory overload.

The most uncomfortable thing about the room was the deafening silence. It hurt. I didn't want to move in my chair for fear the sound of the creaking leather would pierce the room and make the receptionist call for backup. My heart pounded in my chest and I began to think I was stuck in Edgar Allen Poe's *The Tell-Tale Heart*.

As I was redecorating the lobby in my head, I heard some-one turn the handle from the other side of one of the doors and my heart skipped a beat. My breathing became labored and for a second I thought I might pass out. The door opened slowly and to my surprise a beautiful woman with a kind smile peeked through and said my name. Relief filled my body. Neither she nor the individual accompanying her looked like they were going to chop me up into small pieces and hide my remains in a secluded spot, never to be seen again. They both were very kind and compassionate. They escorted me through the hallways and after several turns we entered a small room with two chairs on one side of a desk, one chair on the other, and a suspicious mirror strategically placed on the wall. Nothing else was in that room except the five simple pieces of office furniture doused in bad fluorescent lighting. It took everything in me not to look into the mirror and wave, knowing someone just had to be in a room behind it watching our every move and writing down my every word.

Actually, I imagine my words were being recorded, so the mystery person behind the mirror could just observe. I had to take a deep breath and slow my mind before I screamed profanity strictly out of fear.

The woman, the one I had spoken to on the phone less than twenty-four hours before, introduced herself and gestured with her arm that I should sit in the lone chair on the other side of the desk. As I got *un*comfortable in my seat, they each pulled out a legal pad from their briefcases and twisted the bottom of their expensive Mont Blanc pens. I tried my best not to stare at the lanyards that hung from their necks. The cheap plastic was a stark contrast to their expensive, perfectly pressed and tailored suits. From my seat I could clearly see that each lanyard held their badge, accompanied by a photo, name, and "FBI" in huge letters.

There was no mistaking where I was, and I had to stifle the giggle I could feel rising to the surface. Oh heavens, why was I about to start laughing?

*Lord, please don't let me laugh right now.*

Nothing about this was funny. It felt like a bad episode of *CSI*, and I had somehow found myself on the wrong side of the interrogation table. For some reason that made me want to laugh—or cry. Was it funny that I was being interrogated by the FBI or was it sad? I didn't know, but either way I had to keep my composure.

I couldn't make sense of how I had ended up there, sitting in that small room with two FBI agents questioning me about my father and his computer. He was dead after all, and I just wanted to read his emails. A simple phone call asking for his computer from the evidence room at the police station led to a chain of events that put me in that seat. My obsessiveness has always gotten me into trouble, but I could talk my way out of almost any situation. I learned that from my dad. This time was different. I was stuck, and no amount of smooth talk was going to get me out of that room any quicker than I had gotten in. These people had obviously dealt with my dad before, and perhaps thought that somewhere deep inside of me I was like him. I chose to take the path of least resistance and gave simple and honest answers. I figured trying to talk my way out of that room would only show that I was like him, something I had fought for years to prove otherwise.

I wasn't the criminal. I wasn't then and I'm not now, but I have always worried that somehow I would be the one to pay for the crimes my dad committed. The burden of his sins stressed me out my entire life. I took ownership of it and carried it around until my back ached and my arms cramped. I felt that people could just look at me and see that half of me was rotten and half of me was something different. There was a part of me they could easily love, but there was also a part of me they feared. I've known my whole life that I possessed something few others did. For many years I thought I had been blessed with my dad's gift of gab, but I learned through life that it was actually a form of manipulation. My whole life I've dreaded checking the mail for fear of what was in it, or answering the phone for fear of who was on the other end. The moment my last name left my lips I could see people's faces twist like they had just bitten into sour candy and desperately wanted to spit it out. The questions would start immediately and my stomach would begin to ache. After awhile I pretended not to be his daughter. I acted like I didn't know who he was when asked, and I dreamed of the day I would get married and drop my last name.

After years of denial and avoiding my connection to him, I now found myself sitting in front of two FBI agents, stating my name, including my maiden name, and admitting that I was his daughter. It didn't bother me as much anymore. He was gone and could no longer gloat in the fact that I had to call myself his. My quest to be a daddy's girl had led me to that seat. All I ever wanted was for him to tell me that I was good, that I was valuable, and that nothing in his life was more important than I or my siblings. All I ever wanted was his approval, his love, and his honesty. Sitting in that seat I knew without a doubt that day would never come. I was never going to be a daddy's girl. He was never going to cherish me, and he was never going to whisper quietly in my ear, "You matter." It was all over and my chances of that were gone.

The day before my meeting with the FBI, my brother and I drove to the police station to retrieve the items my dad left behind in his hotel room. Those weren't things that weighed on my brother. He didn't require details to process what had happened, and I knew he didn't want to hear all that our dad had done leading up to his suicide.

That's where my brother and I were different. In order for me to begin to understand, I needed details. That started with getting my hands on the items he'd left behind, but I needed my brother's help. As the oldest, he was the next of kin. The police wouldn't release anything to me. He begged me not to go because he didn't want me obsessing over all the details of our dad's suicide. I begged him to go because I was obsessing over it and needed his help. He caved. He caved because he loves me and knew that it would consume every minute of my life if I didn't get to the bottom of it. He caved because I'm his little sister and he's watched my desperate attempts to gain our dad's love our entire lives; maybe this was the one last thing he could do to help me get what I needed from our dad. He caved because he felt responsible for me. He caved not out of weakness but out of love.

I almost felt guilty when we finally made our way to the detective's desk and started going over the list of items they recovered from the room after removing my dad's lifeless body. The detective nonchalantly went down the list as if he were reading a grocery list to his wife. I listened with intent ears as if he were reading from the Bible the very moment Jesus gave his life for me. My brother walked away.

One black briefcase
Two pairs of reading glasses
One walking cane
One flannel shirt
One vapor cigarette
One black leather wallet with contents
One receipt from Home Depot

I squirmed in my seat knowing that I shouldn't ask what was on my mind. I knew to keep my mouth shut but I couldn't, and I prayed that my brother had walked far enough away to not hear me quietly ask if the receipt was for the item my dad used to hang himself. The question flew out of my mouth before I had time to negotiate with my brain all the consequences of knowing the answer. Out of the corner of my eye I saw my brother pacing but I hadn't been brave enough to actually turn my head and make eye contact with him.

My brother's voice boomed over the voices in my head and made me shrink. "What does it matter? Why do you care?" He scolded me because he knew every question I asked was another stab in my heart from our dead father. His voice was crippling and heartbreaking, and I didn't want to hear it. I wanted him to shut up and let me be the crazy daughter who was drilling the detective for more information.

I almost told him to shut up and go sit in the car if he didn't like it. But I needed his signature and, honestly, I knew he wasn't trying to hurt me. He was trying to stop the hurt, to finally, once and for all, end the pain that our father had inflicted on us. Deep inside, he was hurt too. We just showed it differently. Maybe I shouldn't have asked what was on that receipt, but it was too late. The detective was already punching his keyboard to see what was purchased on that rainy Monday afternoon when my dad stole every ounce of worth from me.

I'd been right. The single item on that receipt was my dad's weapon of choice. Knowing it didn't take away any amount of pain. Instead, it filled out the picture in my head when I tossed and turned at night trying to figure it all out. A three-quarter-inch red tow strap that had been cut at one end gave me enough ammunition to fire bullets into my heart every single night for years. That tow strap gave me endless sleepless nights when I would hide in my bathroom with a towel over my mouth so my husband wouldn't hear me wailing in the other room. More than once that tow strap caused me to pull my car over to the side of the road so that I could cover my face and sob so hard I would eventually vomit. That tow strap is the reason it took me two years before I could step foot in a Home Depot. That tow strap is the main villain in my worst nightmare. However, that tow strap wasn't what I had been looking for in the items on the list.

The vapor cigarette made me laugh. He had always been a smoker. When I was a little girl I wrote him notes begging him to quit. The flannel shirt made me feel like a little girl. I was desperate to bury my face in it. I wanted to hold it up to my nose and smell him. But what I really wanted was his computer and cell phone. I needed to see if it was true that his last communication with anyone was an email to his girlfriend that read, "Tell my kids that I love them."

Were we really his last thought? If we were his last thought, why weren't we enough? How were the images of five innocent children not enough to make him stop? I wondered whether his girlfriend had told me about the email to help ease the pain or whether it was the truth. That's the only reason I'd willingly sat in front of the detective trying to acquire all the items that were left in the hotel.

The list didn't have his computer or his cell phone on it, the two items I was desperate to have in my hands. I questioned him about them and again my brother scolded me for inquiring. After a few minutes on his computer, the detective

161

looked at us and said he had never had this happen before but the FBI had already taken the computer and phone from the evidence room. Neither my brother nor I was shocked, and I think that made the detective uncomfortable. When it came to my dad nothing could shock us anymore. The fact that his belongings were taken by the FBI didn't faze either one of us. My brother may have been relieved and figured this was the end of the road. We could finally let it all go and move on. But he had to have known he was wrong and that my relentless pursuit of answers would not end there. He had to have known that I would push on.

I was silent on the car ride home, while the business card in my pocket felt like it was burning a hole straight through to my leg. The woman whose name and number were printed on the expensive, glossy card held the key to what I needed. My brother asked if I was going to call, even though he already knew the answer. I wished I could have told him no, but it would have been a lie. Of course I was going to call. I was going to call the second he drove out of my driveway and headed home

I could barely see the tailgate of his truck turning off my street when my fingers started dialing her number. I had never spoken to the FBI before. It was both terrifying and exciting. I'm not sure what I expected, but she was a stern yet kind woman who refused to give up a lick of information about my dad's computer. Instead, she politely insisted that I come into the office the next day to talk to her. The control freak in me wanted to keep her on the phone and get as much information out of her as I could, but she was good, really good, and dominated the conversation so that I had no opportunity to manipulate her into giving me answers.

I hung up the phone and sat there in shock. I had dialed the number with the intent of getting what I wanted. Instead I was holding an address that would lead me to the FBI building the next day where I would give up answers rather than get them. My dad had somehow won again.

So here I was, sitting across from two FBI agents making my brain weed through all the information in my head to find the answers that matched the questions they were asking.

The agent I'd spoken with was elegant yet strong, and everything about her was polished and seamless. Were we polar opposites or deep down inside would she get me? Was her daddy her hero or had she craved his affection the way I had craved my dad's? Either way we were face-to-face, and I wasn't the one in control. She had the wheel; I had prayers.

During our phone conversation I had mentioned to her that I was worried people would think I had the computer. I was worried that someone might come looking for it and that I would be responsible for putting my family in danger. That might have seemed odd to anyone else, but I guess she already knew there was danger attached to the computer, because I could hear her jotting notes. It was no surprise that her first question to me in that interrogation room was who I thought might want to get their hands on my dad's computer.

*ME!*

*I need to see it.*

*I need to peek inside just to catch a glimpse of his last email and then you can have it back.*

That would have set off all sorts of red flags and possibly sent me into another strange and uncomfortable room. She already knew I wanted it or I wouldn't be sitting across from her. That's not the answer she was looking for, so I told her what she wanted to know.

I offered a list of three names:

His lawyer.

His girlfriend.

His best friend/worst enemy.

The moment I said the name of his best friend her head perked up. It hit me that she knew who he was and my stomach turned.

So that's why I was here. Of course it wasn't about me; it never was when it came to my dad. It had always been about his scheming best friend and whatever it was they were cooking up together. It made me hate both of them even more than I had before, if that was possible. I wondered if he knew my dad was dead, and I wished I could be the one to tell him. The pure evil half of me wanted to see him hurt and squirm like a snake.

When I realized that she knew my dad's best friend and was interested in what I knew about him or why he wanted my dad's computer, I felt a small bolt of power shoot through me. Up to this point she had what I wanted, but now I held a piece, if only the size of a mustard seed, of what she wanted. I would have dropped to my knees and prayed again for the courage of David and mumbled something under my breath about slings and stones, but out of fear I remained in my seat and silently cried out to God.

*God, I don't know the reason you sent me here, but I know you were here before me. Will you please let this be the end? Just help me give them what they want and release me completely from all of this mess he created. None of this belongs to me. I don't want it. I don't want any of it. Release me. Set me free. I can't carry the weight of his sins. I can't even carry the weight of mine. In Jesus's name, Amen.*

A slight smile appeared on my face, and she mirrored it on hers. I took a deep breath in and exhaled. His name and his sins fell out of my mouth and slammed onto the desk in front of me. It was as if they had weighed me down for long enough and were now being regurgitated for someone else to deal with. I got it out, all of it. I told them every piece of information I knew about my dad and his best friend and it felt good. Oh, how I wish he could have sat in that room and begged me to keep quiet. If he had, I would have spoken louder just for effect.

As I spewed information they wrote frantically. I included the day he sinned against me and every detail I could remember of him. I was out of breath by the time all the information had traveled from my mouth to their legal pads, and I sat back with a sigh of relief. I wanted to yell, "Mic drop!" and walk out, but the fear of being handcuffed kept me on a level of sanity. I simply told them that was everything I knew.

At the end of the conversation, or interrogation depending on how you look at it, they told me that I could retrieve the computer in a few weeks from the police detective I spoke to at the police station the day before. That made me laugh out loud, and in my most smart-mouthed way I asked them why I would want the computer after they wiped it clean. It would be useless to me then. The male FBI agent, who had said very few words while sitting on the other side of the desk that day, gave me a grin and let me know that they would just take what they needed off the computer and give the rest back. I rolled my eyes completely out of reflex. We both knew the computer would just be a shell when they were done with it. I told them no thanks and hoped we were done.

The two FBI agents led me back down the hall to the lobby, thanked me for my time, and shut the heavy wooden door behind me. I turned in my visitor's pass, retrieved my driver's license from the stiff receptionist, and signed out. This time my signature was sturdy and straight; my hands were as precise as a surgeon's because I had left all my fear back in that small interrogation room. Those two detectives could have it if they wanted it. I no longer owned it.

I had to be buzzed back out the front door. When the buzzer went off this time, I noticed my heart didn't skip a beat. I pushed the door open with a newfound confidence that hadn't existed two hours before when I had reluctantly walked through that very same door. If I hadn't had boots on I would have skipped down the sidewalk. I wanted them to see my joy just in case they were watching out a window. As I walked past the security guard, through the metal detector, and out into the land of freedom, I waved at him and told him to have a great day. I got nothing in return and relished in it.

You can't get me.

You can't steal my joy.

I'm free!

As I made the long hike across the parking lot back to my car, I started to hear the bricks crash onto the asphalt. One by one, the bricks that had taken so many years to stack up around me came tumbling down, crumbling in my path. I left a wake of rubble behind me, and all the demons from my past could no longer follow me. The claws that once dug into my spine were now desperately clawing through the bricks behind me, desperate to reach me and feed off of me like they had done for years. All those years of hiding behind a wall of shame and guilt were made new. I no longer owned the sins of my father. His rejection no longer had an effect on me. By the time I reached my car, I was a thousand times lighter than when the cold weather had stolen my breath away hours before. I could breathe again.

I unlocked my car door and slid into the driver's seat. It wasn't until I started the car and felt the heater blast my face that I realized just how cold it was outside. The healing in my heart had overwhelmed my mind and blocked out the feeling of the winter wind on my face. I would no longer allow anything to steal my breath again.

I sat in my car for what seemed like an eternity. I couldn't put the car into drive. I couldn't take my eyes off the building in front of me, the building I had feared only two hours before.

It all hit me at once and I felt a tear stream down my face and crash onto my pants. When it landed on my leg, I flinched and looked down to see the wet spot it had left. Then I felt another and soon my legs were nearly soaked with my salty tears. You could almost hear my tears, like waves reaching the shore. It wasn't relief or pain that released the emotions; it was a mixture of pity for my dad and guilt for my freedom. I was sobbing, unable to navigate my car through foggy eyes, so I just sat there and let myself drown in my own little ocean.

Up to this point in my life, I would have given anything to change what I had been through. I prayed on several occasions for God to take it all away. On more than one occasion I even begged him to take me home to heaven. I once texted my husband and told him I wished a Mac truck would slam into me on my way home and disintegrate everything about me. It made me cry harder for the lost little girl I had held on to for so long. All my life I felt like I never truly measured up to the people around me. I was good at things I attempted and usually excelled in anything I put my heart into, but deep inside I always felt like I was second-rate. I always felt like my boyfriends didn't really like me and then that my husband wasn't truly in love with me. I've heard that is called having "daddy issues." I felt like no matter what I did there was no real value in me.

But on this day, sitting in the car only days after my own dad took his life, I felt free from it all. The battle over wanting him in my life and never wanting anything to do with him was over. I was left with two options: I could let it go and forgive him or live the rest of my life heavy with rejection and worthlessness. While in some ways it felt like he still had the final say, I had the choice to forgive or not.

I had spent a great deal of time praying for God to heal me, praying that he would teach me how to not only accept that everything had been part of his plan but also forgive the mess I went through along the way. God had always made it clear that I was to forgive the same way that I had been forgiven. It was only through him that I was able to move forward and find a healthy way to live my life. I choose forgiveness on a daily basis. I choose Jesus every morning.

Sitting in the car that day I made a promise that I would allow myself to mourn the loss of what I had always pretended not to need. I allowed myself to mourn never being loved by my dad. I released the shame and guilt that came with rejection. From that day on I was going to love myself enough to be free of the chains in which I had wrapped myself so long ago. From that day on I would have the courage to forgive others and myself for the sins in our lives. From that day on I was going to truly accept that Jesus died not only for me and my sins but also for my dad and his, and for that reason alone I knew we were both free. From that day on I would embrace that my heavenly Father had always considered me Daddy's little girl—his little girl.

# TWELVE

# My Redemption Song

Life has a funny way of exposing the past and offering up the truth. I've always wanted to hold my pain and secrets tight to my chest. I would have been satisfied taking my hurts to the grave with me, but God always had a better plan. After giving my life to Christ, I began to understand that God has a plan for us and that even through our deepest pain, his plan is always beautiful. Becoming a Christian and truly surrendering my life didn't mean that I wasn't going to continue to face heartache and hurts; it did mean that I would have someone who would carry me through them. I started to accept that the dirt on my feet would be what God would use to help me lead others to him. It gave me the opportunity to show others that even though my feet were dirty, my path leads to Jesus. In this short time on earth that we've been given, that's truly all that matters.

After my dad's funeral, when the dust settled and everyone went on with their lives, my feet still felt stuck. I remained silent and hid my tears behind the door of my bathroom in the dark of the night. Every time I got in my car I would listen to the song that was played at my dad's funeral. I set the player to repeat and as long as I was in my car, that song was playing. I repeated his eulogy in my head several times a day; I knew it by heart. Even though Brandon knew my pain, I felt like I was suffering through life alone. How could anyone possibly understand how I felt or what my heart was going through? How was I ever going to get over what had happened and move forward?

I spent many nights begging God to help me understand why this had happened in my life and how he was ever going to use it for good. My pit seemed to be bottomless. Even with a strong Christian family and strong faith, I was beginning to think God had made a terrible mistake. Had he picked the wrong person to put on this path? Why did he allow me to be the rejected little girl? Whoever coined the phrase "God only gives you what you can handle" is a liar. Life gives you more than you can handle, and that's why we need God. In the midst of my pain and pleading, he started putting my biggest hurts back in front of my face and making me come to terms with them. He taught me to forgive. In fact, God somehow gave me that strength in abundance; forgiveness wasn't a problem for me. My pain was in the feeling of worthlessness. I forgave with ease; why couldn't my heart heal at the same pace?

A few days after my dad had taken his own life, I was with a coworker who knew my story inside and out. We had spent several hours in the car with each other each day and shared our stories. She knew my struggles. We pulled into a shopping center to get our boss a gift card at a local barbershop for Christmas. As we pulled into a parking spot I glanced to my left and saw his car. The man who had sinned against me twenty years ago was parked just a few spots away. I gasped for air so loudly that it spooked my friend. My instinct to run and hide took over and we made our way into a store nearby, a store I was sure he would never enter.

My sweet friend hunkered down next to a shelf of hair dye and held my hand. She knew my fear was overwhelming. Instead of trying to talk me down, she supported me by hiding alongside me. She could tell by the way my eyes fixated on the front of the store that my fear was more than she could help with.

"Are you okay?"

"I don't think so. I don't know what to do."

The bell on the door handle rang, and I knew someone had walked in. I slowly scooted back, making sure I was protected behind the bottles and brushes. I heard his voice, a voice etched in my mind, and realized he had come in too and was up front talking to the cashier. I stopped breathing so that I could try to make out what he was saying, but I couldn't hear. I would have to get closer and I was too scared to move. My friend could see the look on my face and decided to de-escalate the situation for me since I was frozen in fear. She pulled my hand and we almost ran out the door, completely undetected by him. We snuck into the next store, and my body shook like a wet dog.

Here I was, twenty years later, a grown woman, a wife, and a mother, and still completely in fear of the one who had crushed my dignity so long ago. How had he held this power for so long? How was I still his emotional puppet? I frantically pulled my phone from my purse and struggled to work the buttons with shaky hands. I called my aunt and told her what was going on. She knew the man I feared, but she didn't know why I feared him. She knew that he was my dad's best friend and that neither were good people, but she didn't know how much he had damaged me. I simply told her that he was near and I was panicked. She assumed his sin against me was emotional from being an accomplice with my dad. I was hoping that she would tell me to get back in my car, rev the engine, and run him over when he emerged from the store. But she didn't. She calmly told me that maybe, just maybe, this was God's way of allowing me to let it go and forgive the man and the sin that consumed me. Maybe this was God's way of freeing me. Maybe this was the beginning of my redemption song. I knew she was right but couldn't imagine facing this man, so I went back to my car to collect my thoughts and pray that God might give me the courage to make brave choices.

I sat in silence in the front seat, waiting for him to come out of the store. I had no idea what I was going to do or if I was going to do anything at all. I watched as tiny specks of rain began to cover my windshield and the blast from the heater danced on my face. I wasn't thinking. I felt completely blank with zero emotions. For once, I was empty and without a plan.

And then I saw him.

He confidently marched out of the store with a bag dangling from his arm and headed toward his car. I paused for a moment and in the second of the pause my friend asked me what I was going to do. I didn't answer. With a courage that wasn't mine, a courage that I borrowed from my heavenly Father, I got out of my car and walked up to him. I yelled his name as I approached, and he turned around with a confused look.

"Who are you?"

He didn't know me. He didn't recognize my face. A flood of emotions didn't rush through his entire body the way they had done in mine. He hadn't been locked in the same cage I had locked myself in.

*Who are you?*

That one sentence felt like a bomb in my stomach. How did he not immediately know who I was? How had my face not been etched in his memory? I realize I wasn't the sixteen-year-old girl he had stolen from and that my face showed years of aging. But his face had never left my memory. I thought mine had never left his.

"Candice Snell."

I used my maiden name so he would be sure to make the connection, and I prayed that the very mention of my name would be like a baseball bat to the face. I used my dad's last name for a little extra sting.

"Candice," I said again.

I saw it in his eyes the moment it clicked, and he realized who it was standing in front of him. He looked down, took a deep breath, and then he cried.

I lacked any compassion. I couldn't have shed a tear if you sprayed me with pepper spray. That was his fault. That's what he had stolen from me as a child. He single-handedly took any tears I might have had for him twenty years ago.

He mentioned my dad and cried harder as we talked about his death. He'd already known about it, but as I laid out the details he became more and more upset. My dad had held some weird special spot in his life, and I knew he had just lost one of his best friends. I had a hard time sympathizing with him and did absolutely nothing to comfort him in the midst of his pain. I was over sacrificing myself to help him. I wasn't going to cower, not this time. I lifted my head a little higher and set my shoulders back an inch or two in an effort to state my position. I was not a weak child any longer.

Then, like a kind and gentle man, he told me about his daughter. His eyes sparkled as he said her name, and my whole body went numb. God had let this man become a father. He didn't consult with me or ask me if it was okay; he just gave him a child. Not only was he given a little girl but he was so proud of her. He beamed at the mention of her name, and I was jealous. I was jealous because she had in her dad, the man whom I feared, what I was desperate for in mine. A little girl admired and loved this man, and I knew in that moment I had to end it all. I had to stop the cycle and let it all go. I couldn't live my life hating someone who was deeply loved by his daughter and by my heavenly Father. He was no different from me in God's eyes. Our sins held equal weight, no matter how I felt about it. God gave his Son for this man the same way he gave his Son for me. I knew, right then and there, that I had to forgive the one person in my life that I had promised myself I would hold a grudge against forever. In an effort to do right by his daughter and to somehow be an example of a godly woman for her, even if she never saw it, I forgave her dad.

"I forgive you. I don't hate you anymore, and I will never spend another day of my life hating you."

He simply said, "I'm sorry," as tears rolled down his face.

I hadn't realized that it was now pouring rain. I was soaked and so was he. His face was soaked in tears and mine in raindrops.

God had washed us both clean and it was over. It was time to move on and let it go.

# THIRTEEN

# The Power of Forgiveness

God opened my eyes that day and gave me a sneak peek of what he can do in our lives when we surrender to his will and let go of our own. That day began a rolling redemption in my life that can only be explained by the hand of my heavenly Father. That day God whispered in my ear, "Share your story and I will redeem it all."

Because of what God did that day, Brandon and I decided to give everything we had to the Lord and submit to his plan for our lives. It was a crazy choice and a difficult one, because we were still struggling to recover from all the hits we had taken over the years. We had faced empty bank accounts, sick children, a marriage that hit rock bottom, and deaths in our family that rocked our world. But we had the choice to either continue living our lives for the world and what little it had to offer or fully submit to the Lord and willingly follow where he led. We chose to find God's hand in all that was happening in our lives and all that would happen in the future. We made the choice to completely forgive the past failures in our marriage and not make either of us live a life sentence for them. That meant forgiving cold hearts, infidelity, harsh words, and all the other things that had almost brought our marriage to an end. We left them in the past and never pulled them back out to use as weapons. From here on, no matter how tough things got, I would not bring up the infidelity and swing it wildly like a sword in battle. It was over, forgiven.

It would take more courage and faith than we had anticipated, and it was a taller order than we had ever dreamed. We knew God could and would redeem our marriage and rebuild our family with God as our solid foundation. That doesn't always make things look perfect or pretty, but it makes thing right with God. And we were at peace with that because God's plans are always perfect. We decided to rest in that.

We started by tearing our house down and rebuilding with God as the center of our home. There was no actual deconstruction of our home, but there was a rebuilding in our hearts. We made daily careful and conscious choices to choose differently than we had in the past. For the first time, when faced with life decisions, we paused and consulted our heavenly Father first. For the first time in our marriage, we prayed together. For the first time in our lives, we prayed for God's will to be done and the courage to accept it.

We never thought that the first blessing in submitting to God would be the gift of a precious baby boy. In 2013, a pregnancy test showed a plus sign. We would be adding another child to our home that already had four sweet girls in it.

My husband was sitting in his recliner after work, relaxing from a hard day, and even though we wanted another child and had given the plan to God, I was still nervous about telling him.

"You know how we said we would give everything to God?"

"What happened?"

"Well, I'm pregnant."

"That's awesome."

"Are you mad?"

"Not at all. Why would I be mad?"

I wish I could capture in words the look on people's faces when we told them we were pregnant again. But we had no doubt it was a perfect gift and exactly what God had planned for us all along. It's funny how when we make the kind of life change that we had, everything seems to make sense and not make sense all at the same time.

A month before our son was born, my stepdad, the man who filled the gaps left by my father and garnished my neck with three diamonds and a single pearl, fell severely ill from the flu. I wasn't allowed to visit him because I was pregnant, so we prayed while mom sat by his hospital bed day in and day out.

On January 20, 2014, my heavenly Father welcomed home the father I cherished on earth. For the second time in my life, I lost a father without getting to say good-bye.

While the loss of the man I considered my dad was devastating, I had a peace that I had never known before, a peace that can only come from knowing God. We mourned him deeply, but I never doubted God's hand in the situation. I cried for my mom and the changes she would face, but I was at peace with his passing.

As we were leaving his funeral, my husband took my hand and asked if I would be okay with changing our son's name from what we had already selected to my stepdad's name. Exactly a month later we welcomed baby James Emory into our family. He was like a perfectly wrapped gift that God gave us to celebrate our renewed marriage and to let us know that our family was now whole. He was the gift of new life after mourning the loss of my stepdad. While we were hurt that my stepdad would never meet his little namesake, we were happy that my husband's dad got to hold him. Just once, my husband's dad held his grandson in the crook of his arm and got to look him in the eyes, and then the Lord called him home. We said good-bye to him in May of 2014. Within a matter of months, our children were without any grandfathers.

## Rolling Redemption

God whispered again, "Share your story and I will redeem it all."

It takes extreme faith to open our hands to the Lord, knowing he will take things out of them that we hold dear. For many years we held a tight grip on things in our lives that were separating us from God. We needed to have faith that whatever God removed, he would replace with blessings that would nurture our relationship with him. He began to fill our hands with unexpected gifts.

Neither my husband nor I had a solid childhood home. It was always a dream of ours to raise our children in the same house their entire lives. I moved seventeen times before

I graduated from high school and many times since. My husband grew up much the same way, bouncing from house to house. We desperately wanted our children to have a childhood home filled with the memories of the best hiding spots, the loss of a first tooth, slumber parties, birthday celebrations, a first kiss, and so many other milestones. We wanted them to have a home they could return to year after year and bring their children to.

My favorite place growing up was my best friend's house. We met when we were six years old and became instant friends. She's my safe place, my comfort zone, and I spent a good part of my childhood hanging out at her house.

When Brandon and I first got married we drove by the house, and I told him that it was my dream home. It wasn't a mansion set back among rows of trees. It wasn't a ranch with acres of land to roam. But it was like home to me. The kitchen smelled of fresh brewed tea and the living room had a family feel. The door was always opened for me, welcoming me in to eat dinner and play for hours on end. The walls contained my giggles. My best friend's bedroom held countless secrets that we had whispered to each other over the years. Her home was deep in my heart.

When we started to look for a new home for our ever-growing family, nothing satisfied my need to truly call a house our home. None of the houses we looked at begged me to raise a family there.

One sunny afternoon I met my best friend for lunch, and we went over the houses we had looked at. None of them felt like they were the right fit for my family.

My best friend had lost her dad the year before and had been faithfully keeping up his home, which had sat empty since his passing. The home she grew up in, the home that I had spent countless nights in as a child, the one that had been my safe place so many times growing up, was sitting empty.

"Why don't you move into my parents' house?"

"I don't want you to feel weird with us living there."

"I would rather you live there than anyone else. I would rather have someone who loves it living there."

When she handed me the keys to her old home and my new home, another piece of my heart was healed. She handed me the keys to the home I had my first sleepover in when I was only eight years old, where we brushed each other's hair long into the night and swam for hours on end every summer. It was where I got ready for prom and had my first kiss. She handed me the keys to her childhood home and gave us the perfect place to raise our children and, God willing, a place where our grandchildren will feel at home too. She blessed us with the opportunity to raise our children in the one place that had always given me complete peace.

## Houses Become Our Homes

God whispered again, "Share your story and I will redeem it all."

On a beautiful March day shortly after my stepdad passed away, my phone rang. On the other end was my mother, sobbing. Her heart was broken, and she was emotionally lost inside the very home that they had vowed to live out the rest of their lives in. They had picked the perfect place for just the two of them and filled the many acres with horses, dogs, and beautiful landscape. My mom would sit in the kitchen and watch my stepdad through the window as he cooked dinner on the grill or warmed his hands by the fire pit. Together they spent many hours planting a garden and watching together as the fruits of their hard work made their way above the carefully placed soil. They were never supposed to leave the place they lovingly made their home.

I could hear the desperation in my mom's voice that day. I knew that the home she had once loved had now become a place of mixed emotions. She clenched it tight in her fist, not wanting to let go, but she could no longer stay. Not only was the land too much to care for but the places inside that had once been safe were now places of pain.

We reluctantly agreed that she should sell and move closer to me so that she could be near family and have extra hands to help when needed.

A neighbor at our new home had lived in the same house for almost thirty-six years. He remembered me from all those years ago playing in the cul-de-sac with my best friend, running around the yard, and jumping into the pool, squealing at the cold temperature. He was excited to see life back in the house and smiled from ear to ear as a new generation filled up the cul-de-sac. Every day he sat in his driveway and watched my husband work in the yard while the kids played. Every once in a while he would move his chair closer to where my husband was working and say, "I'm not much help with the work, but I can keep you company." When ice cream was on sale he would always buy two, one for him and one for our kids. Our first Christmas in our new home he bought all of our children a new blanket and let them come pick out a special figurine from his collection. He made our kids feel important and special, and they made him feel young again. He would take our trash to the curb on trash day because "pretty girls shouldn't have to deal with the trash."

One day as I pulled into the garage I saw him slowly approaching the car. He patiently waited for me to unload all the kids and then asked to speak with my oldest daughter. He sweetly asked her if it would be okay if he went to her high school volleyball games and cheered her on. She gladly told him that she would love it, and as she headed into the house he reached out for my hand.

"Your husband told me that you both lost your dads this year. I would like to go to her games as a grandfather figure and cheer her on since she no longer has her grandfathers."

I fought the lump in my throat and smiled. It was all I could do; my words were completely lost. He faithfully attended every game and let everyone in the stands know that he was there to cheer for all the girls, but #13 was his special girl. He didn't get around easily, and I know by the time he got from the car to the stands, his knees ached more than he would admit. I told him many times that he didn't have to go to the games if he wasn't feeling well, but he wouldn't hear of it. He made his way to the gym for every home game and stood in the gap for her grandfathers in heaven.

God whispered again, "Share your story and I will redeem it all."

There wasn't a doubt in my mind that God had orchestrated every detail of our lives to bring us to this moment. He showed us that redemption is always around the corner and his grace is always present, even when we are stuck knee-deep in the mud.

One night, I woke in the middle of the night to make the baby a bottle. When I reached the kitchen, I could see emergency vehicle lights pulsing through the window of our front door. I pressed my face to the glass, saw an ambulance at our neighbor's house, and rushed to wake my husband. Before either of us could get to his house, the ambulance was already on the road with him in the back. He had suffered a heart attack in the middle of the night and was never able to come back to his home after that. His presence outside, sitting in his driveway and making sure the cul-de-sac was safe, had become a fixture for us. It was hard to accept the fact that he would no longer be there. His wife had passed away in that home, and he found immense peace in being in the place where she left him to go to the Lord. Together they had taken great pride in their home, and every detail in the house had their own special touch. I knew the decision for him to move was out of necessity and not want. He had no choice but to abandon the home he thought he would live out the rest of his life in. He needed to be closer to family and have extra hands to help when needed. While he recovered in the hospital, he sent his daughter to the house to start tying up loose ends and find a way to move him to his new home states away. I made my way over to introduce myself and tell her what her dad had done for my little girl. We exchanged stories of how amazing and selfless he was and what kind of man it took to faithfully attend my daughter's games so that she would have the memories of a grandfather watching her play. She had no idea that her dad had been loving on the children next door and treating them as if they were his own grandchildren. She had no idea that he had sat in the stands of my daughter's volleyball games and cheered her on. In the middle of her stress and worry for her dad, she caught a glimpse of how happy he had been and how he had become an honorary member of my family.

As we both stood there in tears, she told me that he just wanted to walk out of his house with his clothes and be done. Picking through the many years of memories that he had made in the house was too much to handle, and he needed to make a clean cut. She had a look of panic on her face, wondering how she was going to move her dad several states away to live near her and sell his home at the same time. She was tired and defeated. I watched her open her mom's jewelry box, the one that had been sitting for years collecting dust after her passing. She picked up a handful of costume jewelry necklaces and asked if any of my daughters would want to have them. My heart broke for everything she was about to let go of. I grabbed her hand and reminded her of our awesome God and how he always has a plan.

I could hear God's sweet voice whisper in my ear, "Tell her. Tell her your story."

My story began to pour out of me, completely out of my control, and I watched her face as she listened intently. We talked about God's plan being so much bigger than our own and how her dad got to watch me go from the little friend next door to the mom of the little girl for whom he subbed as a grandfather. In the absence of my father, her father stepped in. There was something so beautiful in that and we connected instantly. She learned that in the midst of her struggles to find her dad a new home, I struggled to find a home for my mom. We had come to the same place in our lives at the exact same time, and neither of us could deny the works of our heavenly Father in orchestrating it all. Her eyes began to soften and the corners of her mouth went from turning down on each side to a slight but obvious smile. She gently reached over and put her hand on my arm in a way that let me know everything was going to be okay, for both of us, and she asked me if my mom would want to buy her dad's home.

This moment equally blessed both of our families. While my mom was packing up her house to move next door to her family, our old neighbor was packing his suitcase to move closer to his. Because of God's perfect timing and the heart of the amazing man who loved my family like his own, my mom became my neighbor and the weight of her worries were lifted. She no longer sees my stepdad when she looks out her kitchen window. I know that she would give anything to see him standing by the grill, getting her dinner ready, but now her view is her grandkids running through her yard, giggling uncontrollably. I get to look out my kitchen window and watch her throw a ball to them as they carefully swing at it with a bat. My husband spent many hours planting a garden between our homes, and we all watched together as the fruits of his hard work began to make their way above the carefully placed soil. She often says how thankful she is that she gets to eat dinner with us most nights. She truly doesn't know how thankful we are to have her so close. She still tears up over the loss of her husband and the loss of the home she thought she'd grow old in, but she clearly sees the gift that God gave our family through the pain. God redeems our saddest moments and makes them our biggest blessings.

## Discovering the Little Girl in My Father's Pocket

On one of the most gorgeous days of the year in March of 2015, my sixteen-year-old sister climbed into the backseat of a car with her best friend sitting shotgun and another friend behind the wheel. It was the start of their spring break. They had plans to simply be teenagers and enjoy the beautiful outdoors. Maybe a hike was ahead or exploring back roads in the Texas hill country. They turned onto an old country road and felt the joy of being young and free as the wind blew into the windows and the sun danced on their faces. With what seemed like all the freedom in the world, the driver pushed the gas pedal as far as it could go, speeding through the twists and turns. Within a matter of minutes the car met with an old, sturdy, deeply rooted tree. The car and its passengers didn't stand a chance, and the car burst into flames.

I was in the middle of preparing dinner for my family when I got the call from my stepmom.

"Everything's okay but Victoria has been in a car wreck."

"Where is she?"

"She's been airlifted to the hospital and is already in surgery."

"I'm on my way."

My little sister was in surgery for a punctured lung, four broken vertebrae, and stitches in her head almost completely from ear to ear.

I had known deep in my heart that this day was coming. She had been struggling with our dad's suicide for years and internalizing her pain because it was easier to hide it than to deal with it. She had built up a tough exterior and lived her life pretending that she didn't need anyone's help or sympathy. I knew her battle all too well but was completely helpless in trying to save her. A year after our dad died she began self-medicating with whatever she could get her hands on. The pain was so evident in her eyes that it was almost painful to look at her.

I hung up the phone and turned to my husband who was sitting at the dinner table with knowing eyes. He could tell by my tone of voice and the short conversation that something was terribly wrong.

"It's my sister."

"Go, I got this."

I left the food on the stove and raced to the hospital. On the short car ride there, I begged God to spare her life or to give us the peace that passes all understanding if he chose to bring her home. The truth was, if he called her home none of us would be able to find peace. We had already faced more than we should when our dad chose to leave this life by his own hand. After searching the floors of the hospital for what seemed like hours, I finally found my two younger brothers huddled in a room with their mom. Traces of tears were left on all of their faces, and fresh ones were starting to form. I couldn't decide whether to yell and scream at them or wrap them up and try to comfort them. I knew something like this was coming. She was too out of control and defiant to make wise choices. It wasn't the single act of getting in the car that day that I was angry about; it was a series of decisions that had put her where she was.

My brothers and I did our best to smile at each other and hug without sobbing. Victoria's the baby of the family, the one we all try to protect like lions. She's the one we tried to keep small and not allow to grow up or face the hard parts of life. But here we were, sitting helplessly in a waiting room, unable to see or protect her in any way.

After we settled down and went over the details of what was going on with our sister and what we might be looking at when she got out of surgery, my stepmom leaned in close to whisper something to me. Though the others already knew what she was going to say, she whispered it in an effort to make it not real.

"Her friend didn't make it."

"Oh God, she's just a child. Does Victoria know?"

"Not yet."

The Lord called her friend, the passenger in the car, home the moment they hit the tree. The Lord called her home on her eighteenth birthday. She was celebrating her birth the day she died.

What my family had to face sitting in that room that day was nothing compared to what the other little girl's family was facing in the small room where they gathered. After her surgery, we comforted my sister and once again had to tell her that a precious person in her life had been tragically taken away from her.

My sister recovered from the wounds she suffered in the wreck but not from the loss of her friend. Her loneliness consumed her. No one could possibly understand the dark places in her heart or the burdens that weighed her down. Our efforts to bring sunshine and happiness to her only made her recoil to deeper and darker places. Her addiction spiraled completely out of control within months, and she left us no other choice but to seek help from professionals who understood her pain in ways we couldn't. She spent the summer between her sophomore and junior year of high school many states away from us in a dual diagnosis facility where she was treated for PTSD and addiction. It was a lonely place for a sixteen-year-old. Even though I knew it was the best thing for her, it wrecked my heart to have her gone. I had failed at saving her. Unlike protecting her from our father in his custody hearing, I had no one to save her from this time. She needed saving from herself, and I wasn't capable of doing that for her. She had to face this without me, and as desperately as I wanted to run to her and fix everything that was broken, I left her there.

Her sadness and loneliness brought up old wounds for me. I started to feel resentment for my dad that I thought I had long let go of. This time I wasn't hurt for what he had put me through. I was hurt for what he was putting her through even in his absence. I knew that she was desperate for the true love of a father. I knew she wanted to be loved like a little girl should be loved. It confused and hurt her. She built a wall. I knew the wall all too well. I had built my own and spent many years behind it. I wasn't capable of saving her, but I begged God to give me a way to tear down her wall before it completely destroyed her.

## Full-Circle Redemption

Every day I begged God to help her. I asked him to use me however he needed as long as she would be okay. I didn't know what was going to happen to her or if God even wanted to use me in her recovery. I just wanted her to heal. While she was far away from me, I pulled down the box that held our dad's belongings. I had gone through it hundreds of times. I had gone through it every single day for almost a year after his passing, checking to see if I missed anything. I had his driver's license, social security card, and Sam's Club membership all tucked away in his wallet, the very wallet they had taken from the back pocket of the jeans he was wearing the day he died. I had his autopsy report, a portion of his ashes, and his reading glasses. But something was drawing me back to that box, so I balanced myself on a chair and pulled it down. I thumbed through his death certificate and several other papers that I refused to throw away and came upon his small black wallet. It was soft from years of use and the leather was cracked in several places. My hands shook violently and tears streamed down my face, completely out of my control. It happened every time I went through the contents of what he left behind that day in room 101. My head always told me not to look at them, to put them away and let them be. But my heart needed the closure, and it had failed to get it. I tortured myself with those items more than I should have. Even though I had read every word on every paper, license, or club card, I reread them each time I opened his wallet.

I carefully set his wallet on my desk and got up and shut the door to my office so that my kids wouldn't accidently walk in and see how pathetic their mother is. The wallet was once again heavily weighted in my hand, and I felt something sturdy behind one of the pockets. I pried my fingers in it like a can opener. I felt something that I hadn't noticed before. Barely able to grip it with my fingers, I wedged out a laminated picture. Looking back at me was a set of chubby cheeks and the sweet smile of my sister in her third-grade picture. It made me want to reach through the picture and touch her precious face. I would give everything to erase the years between that picture and now so that she could still wear the innocent smile that didn't know the hurts she would one day face. I couldn't take my eyes off of her face and then, like a ton of bricks, it hit me: I've never been the little girl in my father's pocket.

It's always been my sister.

She's always been the one.

She's his love.

She's his little girl.

My hand once fit inside his pocket, but she's the one that belonged there. My picture wasn't in that worn leather wallet—it probably never was—but I've never been so thankful as I was to see her face that day. She gets to be his little girl forever. Her relationship with him ended with her adoring him and him adoring her. That's her story with him. My story with him looks vastly different, and I'm at peace with that. I don't want her story to mimic mine. I want her to have a story that is more beautiful than anything I could ever write. It gives me great comfort to know that all along he really did have the ability to love his little girl, even if that little girl wasn't me.

It is not me.

It never was.

It is she.

It always will be.

She's the little girl in my father's pocket.

I sat my gentle husband down that night, terrified to even have the audacity to ask him to make a choice that would not only change the dynamics of our family but change our lives on a daily basis. My request carried a heavy weight, and I knew it would take more out of all of us than we would be prepared for. It wasn't going to be easy. It was going to be the right thing, at least for a little girl who needed what we had to offer.

"We have to help my sister. She needs me. She needs us."

"We'll do whatever we need to do."

"But she needs to come live with us."

"Then tell her this is now her home."

"But do we have room for her?"

"We'll make room."

"It's not going to be easy at all; it's going to be very hard."

"We have five kids in our home, what's one more? It won't be easy but it will be what's best for her. Tell her this is her new home."

It's strange to say that my dad's suicide and my sister's fall from grace were perfect timing, but had it happened before Brandon and I knew Christ, nothing would look the way it does now. We wouldn't have the courage or capacity to love and care for my sister. When people find out that my response to my dad's suicide is that it has become one of my biggest blessings, they always look shocked. But it's true. Something happened after that day that gave Brandon and me a new outlook on life. We saw how short it can be and how easily tomorrow can be taken away. It opened our eyes to what happens when you hold a grudge or stand in stubbornness. It changed us. My dad's suicide, although tragic and devastating, gave me courage and taught me how to be a better and stronger person.

After several family therapy meetings and many private one-on-ones with counselors, a mutual and loving decision was made between me and my husband and Victoria's mom and stepdad. We agreed that our home would be her home. We all knew that, for the time being, it would be the best place for her. The day she walked out of rehab, my husband and I became her guardians. At the sweet and vulnerable age of sixteen, my sister unpacked her bags in her new room at our home, the one we vowed to raise our children in.

Even if only for the blink of an eye, for two short years I get to parent my little sister in a way that our father couldn't.

I get to wake her up every morning and see her off to school. I get to listen to her stories at dinner and kiss her goodnight. My husband not only gets to be her brother-in-law, but he also gets to set an example for her of what a father's love should look like. He gets to model the behavior of a husband and teach her what to look for in her husband. Just for a moment, we get to stand in the gap my dad left behind. Each day she gets to look at me for some trace amount of our dad and gets to experience all the good stuff about him in the reflection of my eyes. I get to be the start of God's redemption story in her life, and I thank him every day for the redemption story in mine. I get to raise the little girl in my father's pocket.

# EPILOGUE

God doesn't make mistakes. He takes the hurts and the messes and redeems them to make this crazy life into something raw and usable. Giving my life to him changed everything about me and how I see the world. I'm going to walk through many fires in my life, there's no doubt about it. I lived most of my life with a selfish pride. It wasn't considered cool to claim God as my Father, and I honestly believed he was ashamed of me. I thought I was protecting myself by building a huge wall and not letting anyone see the struggle behind it. I thought I could make it through alone.

But then Jesus.

My sweet Jesus.

How could someone possibly love me so much that he was willing to give his life for me? He knew me the day he took my sins on as his own and willingly carried his cross to the top of the hill. I can't imagine a love like that. I don't possess it for anyone, not myself or my family. I'm incapable of a love like the one he has for me, but I will spend the rest of my life trying to honor it.

I'll never be good enough to be worthy of what he did for me or what he does in my life every day. That's not what being a believer is about. That's a hard lesson to accept. It's almost impossible for me to truly grasp the fact that God can look on me and claim me as his. But he does. He uses my greatest hurts to show others how big his love is. I think that's the most beautiful thing about my life.

I finally came to a place of peace, not because everything all worked out but because there's this strange thing that comes with being a follower of Jesus. I know the path leads to him, and I will gladly embrace the dirt on my feet along the way. It may not be comfortable or smooth walking, but in the end it's worth it. I want to spend the rest of my life honoring God, who chose to use my messes for good. I want to teach my kids to be servants and pour out love where love is needed. I want to take all the years that I spent consumed with my own hurts and somehow use them to help heal the hurts of others.

My worth was never held in my dad's hands, and no matter how hard I tried I was never going to find it here on earth. My worth was always in the palm of my heavenly Father's hands and always will be. Nothing that I went through while trying to sort through my life was a waste. God used every ounce of it to redeem my story and, hopefully, show others what it looks like to be his child.

None of our stories are pointless. None of us are a mistake. None of us are worthless. Every season of our lives serves a purpose. Even when we are walking through the fires of life, his plan is always perfect and always leads to redemption. His love for us is beyond anything we will ever be able to understand here on earth. But it is real, and it is ours.

# ACKNOWLEDGMENTS

Brandon Curry—Thank you for letting me be me and loving me unconditionally. Thank you for trusting me to tell our story and for never trying to edit what our mess looked like. Thank you for being my strong foundation.

Victoria Snell—Thank you for showing me what real strength looks like. Thank you for sneaking peeks at our story and encouraging me along the way. Thank you for letting me tell Dad's story honestly, no matter how painful it may be. Thank you for allowing me to be your sister and stand-in mother.

Heather Knell—You've always been the sunshine in my life. You know my deepest and ugliest scars, and you still tell me I'm beautiful. You praise me even when I haven't earned it. You saw in me what I couldn't see in myself. Over all these years you've never left me. You're my person. I adore everything about you and am so thankful that God gifted you to me.

Lisa Snell—When your best friend becomes your sister and her kids are your niece and nephew, there's no explanation other than God is the coolest. Thank you for letting me kick and scream at you through this entire process. Thank you for never walking away even when my mess was more than most people would accept.

To my kids—I'm just a shell without each of you. You are the reason I can see God in all the little things through life. You are my beginning and end. Thank you for simply being you and giving me my reason to be better.

Jana Burson, my agent—I can only imagine that you get a little nervous each time you put me on a conference call with important people. Thank you for embracing my lack of a filter and need to insert comedy into every detail. Thank you for your unending patience through this entire process and for having complete faith that God's timing is perfect. Together we have seen firsthand how he has worked this whole thing out, and it's been nothing short of amazing. Thank you for taking a chance on the crazy Christian who had a story to tell. I owe you a big bowl of chips and salsa with a side of queso.

Rebekah Guzman, my editor—You have the patience of a saint. Thank you for the massive amounts of grace you have given me and for showing me how to be a better writer. Thank you for not only guiding me through edits but also giving me heavy doses of encouragement along the way. I didn't expect to gain such a talented and loving friend through this, but God is just cool like that.

Baker Publishing—Thank you for letting me share my story. I hope I make you proud.

**Candice Curry** is a born and raised Texas girl. She is Brandon's wife of ten years and together they are raising their children to love the Lord, be kind, and give back. They are the parents of four daughters and a son and, just when they thought they were done having kids, they welcomed Candice's teenage sister into their home as one of their own. Several years ago Candice put her faith in God's plan for her life and gave up her career in sales to stay at home with the children and share her faith through speaking and writing. Her dream is to one day own an ice cream truck and travel around Texas selling ice cream and French fries while spreading her love for Jesus. Candice started her blog, Women with Worth, in 2011 as a form of therapy after losing her dad. She uses her space in the blog world to write about anything and everything that is on her heart.